The United States
and Asia

Potomac Associates

Potomac Associates is a nonpartisan tax-exempt research organization that seeks to encourage lively inquiry into important issues of public policy. Its purpose is to heighten understanding and improve discourse on significant contemporary problems, national and international, by providing a forum for distinctive points of view.

Members of the Board of Directors of Potomac Associates are Arthur M. Dubow, chairman; T. Jefferson Coolidge, Jr.; Edward P. Morgan; Paul H. Nitze; George R. Packard; Timothy Seldes; and William Watts.

This project was funded by The Henry Luce Foundation.

The United States and Asia

Changing Attitudes and Policies

William Watts
Potomac Associates

LexingtonBooks
D.C. Heath and Company
Lexington, Massachusetts
Toronto

Library of Congress Cataloging in Publication Data

Watts, William, 1930–
  The United States and Asia

  Bibliography: p.
  1. Asia—Foreign opinion, American. 2. Public opinion—United
States. 3. United States—Relations—Asia. 4. Asia—Relations—
United States. I. Title.
DS33.4.U6W37   950   81–47711
ISBN 0–669–04729–5   AACR2

Copyright © 1982 by D.C. Heath and Company

Published simultaneously in Canada

Printed in the United States of America

Casebound International Standard Book Number: 0–669–04729–5

Paperbound International Standard Book Number: 0–669–05370–8

Library of Congress Catalog Card Number: 81–47711

*For my brother, Bigelow, whom Asia keeps;
and my wife, Eve, and my children, Evie,
Shelby, Heidi, and Obadiah, whom Asia awaits*

Contents

List of Figure
and Tables

Figure

Tables

Foreword

This is an important and disquieting book about American attitudes toward Asia. It proves how little U.S. citizens know about the countries and peoples halfway around the globe. We cling to our traditional affection for Europe while seeing most of Asia as "crowded, underdeveloped, dirty."

Such stereotypes are especially disturbing as one flies across the Pacific these days. As I write, I am doing just that, riding in a Boeing 747 on a return flight from Singapore to the United States. Singapore itself is one of the most modern nations on earth with its sparkling new buildings, wide clean boulevards, and bustling harbor (the second most active in the world behind only Rotterdam, and way ahead of America's busiest harbor in New York). Around me on the aircraft I see the new face of Asia: smartly dressed businessmen and bankers from Tokyo, Seoul, Taipei, Hong Kong, Singapore, and Manila; families coming to visit relatives or perhaps for permanent residence where they will join the 2.5 million Asian-Americans. Interspersed throughout the plane are clusters of Europeans and Americans who have just been to Asia, in numbers that grow rapidly each year, to do business or to enjoy fresh tourist opportunities.

The aircraft symbolizes a brand-new era in Asia and Asian-American relations. It takes you to an Asia full of surprises. All of East and most of Southeast Asia is rushing pell-mell after Japan (now the world's second biggest economy) and growth rates of 6–10 percent per year are commonplace throughout the region. Superb products flow out of Asia, ranging from high-technology electronics to high-fashion designer jeans. In many places, new agricultural techniques have wrought rural transformations to parallel those in the pulsing urban centers.

Of course Asia has its serious problems, but they are problems of growth, not stagnation. China, for instance, is struggling to modernize with a total population of over one billion, three-quarters of whom live in the countryside where food production barely keeps pace with population growth. Yet China, in spite of these burdens, has made important strides in recent years and has turned to Europe, Japan, and the United States for commerce and assistance.

Another problem area, also born of success, is that of trade conflicts. The classic example is U.S.-Japanese trade where an American deficit of $15 billion is expected in 1981. American domestic industries, both management and labor, are screaming loudly that Japan and other Asian countries will wipe out everything American from automobiles to textiles.

A third problem area is military. Asia has thousands of miles of hostile border areas and a modern history of prolonged conflicts. The United States, so often drawn into Asian wars in this century, now finds a menacing Soviet Union with a new foothold in Indochina and a beefed-up naval presence in the Pacific.

In a nutshell, Americans face tremendous challenges in dealing with this new Asia. Can we realize the potential in trade, diplomacy, and cultural exchanges? Can we avoid the perils of commercial clashes and military confrontation?

The biggest challenge of all is that of knowledge. Unless Americans bridge the ignorance gap across the Pacific, we are likely to miss opportunities and repeat mistakes. So often we have looked to Asia through Americanized visions and missed what was really happening. The Vietnam War is a case in point. Hawks shouted that Vietnam was merely an extension of China's global appetite. Doves spoke of the beleaguered North Vietnamese who wanted no more than a peaceful nationalism with their own borders. History has proven both sides wrong as China and Vietnam have gone to war and as Vietnam has invaded Cambodia. The lesson is clear: more information and less certitude in our views of Asia. Without it, the results can be tragic.

But where do we start? What do Americans know about Asia? What do they need to know? Here is where this valuable book comes into play. Watts begins with a well-designed Gallup Poll to determine American knowledge and attitudes. Then he goes on to interpret the poll based on his extensive knowledge of polling, of American foreign policy, and of Asia itself. Finally, he offers insightful recommendations for policymakers, businesspeople, journalists, and educators.

Some of his findings are pretty bleak. It appears that many Americans look to Asia the way Hobbes viewed man's natural state: a life that was "nasty, brutish, and short." Americans tend to identify with those Asian nations closest in geography and experience, most particularly with Japan, the Philippines, and Australia. Sadly, we know little of the economic breakthroughs of South Korea, Taiwan, and Singapore, all of which are wrongly seen as behind China in terms of estimates on standard of living. It is also a pity that Americans know so little about the key countries of ASEAN (Association of Southeast Asian Nations), comprising Thailand, Malaysia, Singapore, Indonesia, and the Philippines. ASEAN is a regional grouping of energetic noncommunist countries with great potential in economic cooperation. The ASEAN countries have recently taken the lead in seeking the resolution to the ongoing Indochinese logjam.

Some of Watts's discoveries are surprising. U.S. normalization with the People's Republic of China, for instance, has produced a surge of support for closer U.S.-China relations, a dramatic turnabout from more suspicious attitudes in the mid-1970s. Toward Japan, Americans have evolved a split view of great respect for its industry and great fear for its exports. Curiously, less than a third polled saw the Japanese government as democratic (though the other options in this question may have biased the result somewhat). South Korea still suffers from the bad press of the last decade so that concerns for human rights and corruption continue to overshadow American awareness of Korea's economic vibrancy.

Some of the results are a little more positive. On a quiz of basic information, more than half the population scored a passable grade of five correct answers out of eight. Although the bias remains in favor of Europe, substantial numbers of Americans now recognize that U.S.-Asian trade is now greater than U.S.-European trade.

All this demonstrates that some accurate knowledge about Asia has seeped into the American public at large. To some extent this is due to the hard work of a new generation of Asia experts in universities, government, business, and the media. To some extent it reflects the labors of a small band of outreach coordinators at the universities and teachers committed to upgrading the K-12 curriculum about Asia. It also indicates the impact of a few fine television specials and documentaries, as well as the increased attention to East Asia in the press. Yet the reverse is also true. American ignorance of Southeast and South Asia is due, more than anything else, to the miniscule attention they receive in U.S. print and broadcast journalism.

The bottom line of Watts's book, however, is that we have a long way to go. Most American schoolchildren learn almost nothing about Asia. Most textbooks are still filled with stereotypes and outmoded information. Only 3 percent of college students take any course having any connection to Asia. Foreign-language study is sharply down throughout the United States, and Asian languages capture only a tiny percentage of that dwindling number. One estimate is that no more than 20,000 Americans are studying Chinese and Japanese (compared to a majority of students in China and Japan who are learning English).

What can be done about it? Watts correctly proposes a multifaceted strategy that links the White House, the Hill, Wall Street, Harvard Square, Madison Avenue, the nightly news, and your local high school. Such an effort must focus not only on the Asia over there, but also on the important roles played by Americans of Asian extraction whose numbers have jumped in recent years. Such an effort demands, as Watts indicates, new infusion of government and foundation support (at just the time when everybody is cutting back). Above all, it requires a strong push for understanding Asia by many prominent Americans, ideally the president himself.

Watts and The Henry Luce Foundation have given a good, hard nudge in the right direction.

Robert B. Oxnam
President
The Asia Society, Inc.

Acknowledgments

Many people have helped to make this book possible, and I apologize in advance if I fail to give proper credit where it is due.

Funding for the entire project, including all research, travel, and a special one-day conference held at The Johns Hopkins University School of Advanced International Studies in November of 1980 was provided by The Henry Luce Foundation. I am deeply grateful to Martha Wallace and Rob Armstrong for their immediate and continuing interest, support, and advice. They made it all happen.

I am also grateful to George R. Packard, dean of the School of Advanced International Studies, for his willingness to host the conference at which many of these ideas originated. He and other panelists and speakers, including Winston Lord, president of the Council on Foreign Relations; Robert B. Oxnam, then director of the Washington Center of The Asia Society; Richard Holbrooke, then Assistant Secretary of State for East Asian and Pacific Affairs; Don Oberdorfer, diplomatic correspondent for *The Washington Post;* and His Excellency Zain Azraai, ambassador of Malaysia, contributed enormously to my thinking and conclusions.

It is also a pleasure to be able to acknowledge the faithful support of my board of directors, whose names appear on another page. Their advice and understanding from start to finish of this, and all other Potomac Associates efforts, has been a source of genuine inspiration.

Leonard Wood and Dr. Henry Cotugno of The Gallup Organization were extremely helpful in the design of the questionnaire, and Leonard Wood also gave useful advice on parts of the data interpretation.

Maria Lourdes-Gatmaitan was exceptionally helpful in her diligent research assistance, and in other organizational aspects of the entire effort. Tressie Minor and her colleagues provided much-needed and much-appreciated logistical support. Typing of the original manuscript was carried out with utmost efficiency, under difficult time pressures, by Maryllis Bartlett, Sharon Mee, and Elizabeth Hoopes.

Finally, I wish to thank my many friends and advisors, both here and in Asia, whose thoughts and suggestions have found their way into this undertaking. Since those who were specially interviewed for this book were guaranteed anonymity, I must regretfully leave out their names. They know who they are, and I am happy to express my very genuine gratitude for the extraordinary contribution they have made. Lloyd Free, the man who has taught me most of what I know about survey research, its pitfalls and its uses (and who was not interviewed), can be saluted here, and I am proud to do so. And I am grateful to Robert J. McCoy, who lent his remarkable editorial advice once again.

I hasten to add that the final result is my responsibility alone, and any errors, faulty interpretations, or inappropriate recommendations that have worked their way into the text should not be attributed to anyone else.

Introduction

A comprehensive survey of American opinion, knowledge, and attitudes about Asia, its countries and its peoples, conducted in the summer of 1980, revealed the following:

A majority of Americans believed at that time that the People's Republic of China was one of our fifteen largest trading partners.

A majority said that Indonesia was not a major supplier of oil and petroleum products to the United States.

A majority believed that the United States still provided major economic aid to South Korea.

The majorities were wrong on all counts.

More than three Americans in ten did not know that the Philippines was once an American colony.

Less than one-third thought that the government of Japan was democratic.

The adjectives or phrases that Americans selected most frequently from a varied list when asked about Asia included "crowded; too many people," "underdeveloped," "political unrest," and "dirty; poor sanitation."

Much misinformation and negative stereotypes appear to characterize the thinking of many of our citizens when they turn their minds to Asia today.

Yet think about the following facts:

More than 20 percent of the world's population now lives in China, and about one-half lives in Asia.

Japan has emerged as one of the world's economic superpowers.

U.S. trade with Asia surpassed that with Europe in 1977, and the volume of our commerce across the Pacific is sure to continue to increase.

Immigration of peoples from Asia to the United States has soared, with the number of Chinese in this country almost doubling during the 1970s, the number of Filipinos more than doubling, and the number of Koreans increasing by 413 percent.

The Korean peninsula, where American forces and our national security are clearly engaged, remains one of the most dangerous flashpoints on the globe, with the interests of China, Japan, the USSR, and the United States all directly involved.

Some of the world's most dynamic and rapidly growing economies are located in the region, including those of Singapore, South Korea, and Taiwan.

Asia has one of the most constructive regional organizations in the world, the Association of Southeast Asian Nations (ASEAN).

The last three wars in which the United States was involved began, for us, in Asia.

Given such fundamental realities, virtually all of which have major implications for U.S. policy, both official and nonofficial, it behooves us to become well informed and nonparochial about Asia.

This book deals with the realities of American perceptions of Asia as they now exist and suggests some steps that need to be taken both here, and in those Asian nations that so wish to improve the mutual levels of understanding and intercourse. Our discussion will also deal with some of the most pressing policy issues now before the United States in Asia, and suggest new policy approaches that might be taken.

For purposes of our analysis, Asia has been defined in terms of the Pacific rim, to include the following countries and areas: Australia, Cambodia, the People's Republic of China, the Democratic People's Republic of Korea (North Korea), Indonesia, Malaysia, New Zealand, the Philippines, the Republic of Korea (South Korea), Singapore, the Soviet Union, Taiwan, Thailand, and Vietnam.

The primary body of data has been derived from personal interviews of a nationally representative sample of 1,616 adult Americans eighteen years of age and older, completed July 2, 1980, by The Gallup Organization of Princeton, New Jersey. The results of the survey have been broken down into various demographic groups, allowing for more detailed examination of attitudes according to sex, age, income, race, education, and region of country where one resides, occupation, and level of interest in international affairs.

An additional set of interviews was conducted with forty-seven individuals who have direct, personal contact with one or more countries in Asia and their peoples. Drawn from business, labor, the academic and foundation community, and government (primarily the executive and legislative branches), these people encompass a broad intellectual and professional spectrum. Their views have provided an exceptionally rich resource.

It is my hope that the pages that follow will provide some food for thought, debate, and argument, and perhaps even contribute to the greater understanding, dialogue, and promotion of mutual self-interest that is vitally needed on both sides of the Pacific and that can add to the well-being and security of us all.

1

The Place of Asia in the American World View

Observers of the United States regularly look upon Americans as Eurocentric, and with considerable justification. Most of the early settlers of the land that would eventually become the United States were of European stock, and so our eyes and minds have tended to turn almost instinctively in that direction when we think of foreign affairs and especially of foreign commitments. Given the history of social and cultural links, customs that often are closer to our own and thus more readily understandable, and languages not so remarkably alien (even if we do not bother to learn them, which most Americans are loath to do), it is probably only natural that Europe looms largest on the international horizon for most of us.

Such a bias, however, will no longer do. Other regions of the globe demand our attention with increasing force: Africa, breaking away from its colonial and tribal past; the Middle East, which has oil deposits that are essential for our very existence; Latin America, where countries long taken for granted now insist on their own place in the sun; and Asia, where the largest numbers of human beings reside and where abundant natural resources and burgeoning skills have given rise to the most vital economic region on the face of the earth and the center of several of the world's fastest growing economies.

Overall Importance: Asia versus Europe

That many Americans are reluctant to recognize some of these changes is attested to by responses to a question from the indepth survey of public attitudes in this country toward Asia (also posed in an earlier Potomac Associates study) that will form the backdrop for much of the discussion in the pages that follow:

1

The United States has strong political, economic, and national-defense ties with friendly nations in Western Europe, on one hand, and with friendly nations in and near Asia, on the other hand. Thinking about each of these two areas from the standpoint of promoting our own political, economic, and national-defense interests, which do you think is more important to the United States—friendly nations in Western Europe or friendly nations in Asia?

	1978 (Percent)	1980 (Percent)	Change in Percentage Points 1978–1980
Friendly nations in Western Europe	39	45	+ 6
Friendly nations in Asia	18	19	+ 1
Both about equally important	29	26	− 3
Do not know	14	10	− 4

Overall, the balance among Americans who picked one area over the other is somewhat greater than two to one in favor of Europe, while approximately one-quarter saw Europe and Asia as roughly equal in their importance to U.S. political, economic, and national-defense interests. The modest increase between 1978 and 1980 in those who placed Europe first may well have been a reflection of the heightened concern at the time our survey was conducted over the twin crises of the seizure of American hostages in Iran and the Soviet invasion of Afghanistan. In both of those tension-ridden events, Americans (or the general public, at least) would naturally see support for threatened U.S. interests linked primarily to friends in Europe, tied more closely to us through a tighter web of alliances, and comfortable, long-standing commercial and other networks, rather than to those in Asia.

Among various demographic groups, Easterners were more inclined to rate both areas about equally important, and Europe somewhat less important, than Americans living in the other parts of the country. Nonwhites put friendly Asian nations almost on a par with Europe. This more favorable view of the importance of Asian nations among nonwhites (almost all those interviewed were black, combined with small numbers of Hispanic Americans and others) is probably tied to a generally more sympathetic view of the third world, that is, nonwhite areas of the globe; as we shall see later, blacks tended to hold more favorable views than did whites of many of the nonwhite nations about which we tested sentiments in this survey. (Other studies also show that blacks are regularly more supportive than whites of the United Nations, probably seeing in it a forum for Asian, African, and other nations to express their views to, and make them felt by, the predominantly white major economic powers of the world.)

Those who are "very interested" in international affairs (levels of interest in international affairs were derived by asking individuals whether they read various weekly and monthly magazines and journals that carry extensive reporting on foreign affairs) came out more strongly than the national norm for *both* Europe (51 percent as opposed to 45 percent of all Americans) *and* Asia (33 percent as contrasted to 19 percent of the total). Only 15 percent of the "very interested" rated the two areas as about equal. The extra degree of interest this group displays in international affairs apparently led it to select one geographic alternative or the other and steer away from what may be seen as the less decisive answer in the middle.

Levels of Like and Dislike

Another way to look at how Americans rate nations of Asia in their general world view is by asking them to express levels of like or dislike for specific countries. To this end, we asked respondents in the national survey:

Here is an interesting experiment. [Interviewer hands respondent Scalometer card.] You notice that the ten boxes on this card go from the highest position of + 5—or someone or something you like very much—all the way down to the lowest position of − 5—or someone or something you dislike very much. Please tell me how far up the scale or how far down the scale you rate the following [nations].

The ratings given twenty-one nations around the world, including seven outside the geographic confines of Asia as defined for this project, are presented in descending order in table 1-1. ("Highly favorable" views indicate a rating of + 4 and + 5; "mildly favorable," a

Table 1-1
Levels of Favorable/Unfavorable Attitudes

	Highly Favorable (Percentage)	Mildly Favorable (Percentage)	Mildly Unfavorable (Percentage)	Highly Unfavorable (Percentage)	Do Not Know (Percentage)
1. Canada	75	20	1	1	3
2. Australia	49	42	3	1	5
3. West Germany	33	48	11	4	4
4. Japan	30	54	9	3	4
5. New Zealand	28	55	7	2	8
5. Israel	28	50	13	5	4
7. Brazil	21	60	11	2	6
7. Philippines	21	59	10	2	8
9. China	17	53	18	8	4
10. Saudi Arabia	15	40	23	17	5
11. Taiwan	13	55	20	6	6
12. Singapore	9	57	20	4	10
12. India	9	54	26	6	5
12. Thailand	9	50	26	7	8
12. South Korea	9	50	28	8	5
16. Nigeria	7	47	28	7	11
17. USSR	6	17	27	47	3
18. Indonesia	5	52	26	5	12
18. Malaysia	5	51	23	4	17
18. Vietnam	5	23	35	33	4
21. North Korea	2	24	41	28	5

rating of $+1$, $+2$, and $+3$; "mildly unfavorable," a rating of -1, -2, and -3; "highly unfavorable," a rating of -4 and -5.)

The top six countries—Canada, Australia, West Germany, Japan, New Zealand, and Israel—represent either developed nations or nations with whom Americans are likely to identify through a variety of cultural, social, and historical links. Only one non-Occidental country—Japan—is found in this top grouping; as we proceed through our examination of the survey results, it will become strikingly apparent that Americans, as a group, consistently accorded Japan a very special, and generally very high, place in their overall esteem.

Four nations, it should be noted, were given considerably more "highly unfavorable" ratings than the rest—the USSR, Vietnam, North Korea, and Saudi Arabia, in that order. The first three, in particular, regularly received the lowest marks from Americans, relegating them to a kind of pariah status in our national outlook.

Differences among various segments of the American population in terms of their comparative levels of like and dislike for the Asian countries on our list were not too numerous. Americans who are "very interested" in international affairs gave more positive ratings, especially in the "highly favorable" category, to Australia, China, Japan, New Zealand, and Taiwan, and were even more negative than the average toward North Korea and Vietnam. In the case of the USSR, the "very interested" were marginally less *un*favorable, as were blacks, the college educated, and Westerners (in contrast to the very negative attitudes of Southerners, traditionally a source of more patriotic or nationalistic sentiments).

The eighteen- to twenty-four-year-old age group was slightly more positive than the norm in its "highly favorable" ratings of China, as were blacks. Black Americans, on the other hand, were less positive than Americans in general toward both Australia and New Zealand, probably reflecting a perception of restrictive racial and/or immigration policies in those countries.

Both Japan and New Zealand ranked better than average among Westerners; New Zealand received similarly positive support from members of the professional and business community.

Perhaps the most important finding on this topic is the extent to which attitudes toward many of the countries in Asia are relatively unformed and noncommittal. In the cases of China, Indonesia, South Korea, Malaysia, the Philippines, Singapore, Taiwan, and Thailand, the great bulk of Americans gave ratings in the +1, +2, sometimes +3, and −1 categories—all fairly close to the middle, and probably representing in many instances a rather safe, conservative, and relatively uninformed judgment. Only Japan, Australia, and New Zealand received strong clusters in the +3, +4, and +5 categories, whereas the heavy minuses were reserved for the USSR, North Korea, and Vietnam.

What this finding suggests for the countries in the soft middle is that there is much room for movement in American attitudes—particularly, as we shall see later, in view of the stated and actual levels of ignorance and misinformation about many of these countries.

For some of the countries on our list, limited earlier data are available from the Gallup data bank, and are shown in table 1-2.

As table 1-2 suggests, one of the most remarkable developments over the past few years has been the colossal shift of opinion in Americans' views about the People's Republic of China. The new opening to China and eventual diplomatic recognition of the authori-

Table 1-2
Shifts in Highly Favorable Views

	1976 (Percentage)	1980 (Percentage)	Shift 1976–1980
Canada	60	75	+ 15
Australia	36	49	+ 13
West Germany	22	33	+ 11
Japan	22	30	+ 8
Israel	17	28	+ 11
Philippines	15	21	+ 6
Brazil	9	21	+ 12
China (referred to as "Communist China" in 1976)	3	17	+ 14
Taiwan (referred to as "Nationalist China" in 1976)	9	13	+ 4
India	7	9	+ 2
USSR (referred to as "Russia" in 1976)	4	6	+ 2

ties in Peking have been digested and overwhelmingly approved by our population. If we look at the balance between total favorable views (+ 1 to + 5) and total unfavorable (− 1 to − 5), the following picture emerges, with comparable data included from earlier Potomac Associates studies on Taiwan, Japan, South Korea, and North Korea.

Favorable/ Unfavorable Rating (Percent)	China	Taiwan	Japan	South Korea	North Korea
1977	26–52	56–18	—	—	—
1978	—	—	72–17	52–27	13–65
1979	65–25	64–20	82–11	58–27	29–56
1980	70–26	68–26	84–12	59–36	26–69

What had been a negative margin of two to one against the People's Republic of China in 1977 was completely reversed to a better than two-to-one positive rating two years later, after the United States severed formal diplomatic ties with Taiwan and recognized the People's Republic in January of 1979. And in the following year the favorable trend for Peking had been maintained.

It is also important to note again the very high ratings given

Japan. In spite of genuine concern about the threat of imports from Japan, which is discussed further in subsequent pages, the overall attitudes of Americans remained very high, with no signs of slippage.

Importance to U.S. Interests

In assessing where Americans place Asia and Asian nations in their overall world view, we can point to one other indicator taken from an earlier Potomac Associates study. To determine the perceived importance of getting along with certain countries, we asked:

When it comes to pursuing our interests all around the world, how important do you think it is for the United States to try to get along well with each of the following countries: very important, fairly important, not so important, or not important at all?

Percentages of those who said "very important" are listed in table 1-3.

Geographic proximity and/or perceptions of political, military, and economic muscle set the tone. The USSR, Japan, and China dominated the scene as far as Asian countries are concerned. In this

Table 1-3
Importance to U.S. Interests

	1979 (Percentage)
Canada	76
USSR	67
Mexico	67
Saudi Arabia	63
Japan	58
China	57
Israel	57
Egypt	53
West Germany	54
Cuba	46
Taiwan	44
Australia	41
South Korea	35
Brazil	34
India	33
Nigeria	30
North Korea	29

measure, it should be mentioned, Americans were prepared to put aside some of their dislikes in favor of a realistic assessment of the world scene: both the USSR and Saudi Arabia fared better when rated on the basis of their relative importance to U.S. interests than they did in terms of their popularity.

Asia versus Europe: Voices of Experience

As noted in the introductory section, a key part of this survey of attitudes was a wide-ranging series of interviews with a number of individuals, both in government and out, who have had extended and direct experience in Asia. Bankers, lawyers, businessmen, labor leaders, diplomats, intelligence officials, congressional staffers, White House officials, scholars—their views bring a special richness to this analysis and will be considered as a separate element in later segments of our discussion, wherever appropriate.

It is fitting, perhaps, that on this very first issue—the relative overall importance of Europe as compared with Asia—these individuals with an ability to give a particularly sensitive assessment tended to cluster in the middle:

	Leadership *(Percent)*	*All Adults* *(Percent)*
Friendly nations in Western Europe	24	45
Friendly nations in Asia	13	19
Both about equally important	62	26
No opinion	1	10

Given the extremely small size of this leadership sample (forty-seven persons, chosen on the basis of their reputation, variety of professional experience, and with a conscious attempt to cover the ideological spectrum), the percentage results must be treated with great caution and looked on primarily as indicators. Even taking this caveat into account, however, it remains striking indeed that the clear preponderance of opinion called for treating both areas more or less equally. Where there was an inclination to opt for one region over the other, Europe came out ahead—just as it did for Americans as a whole, as well as for that group of Americans that showed itself to be especially interested in international affairs.

What thinking led this group of specialists to choose so overwhelmingly a more balanced equation between Europe and Asia? Balance is called for, they say, because it makes the most sense, because it is most in tune with today's world realities, and because it corresponds most closely to the best interests of the United States. The past place of pride given to Europe no longer conforms to the relative weight the two areas hold in U.S. trade, for example (with the totals across the Atlantic and Pacific Oceans now close to equal, but with Asia clearly forging ahead to a position where it will be our dominant regional partner in the future), or security interests (for the United States, our last three major wars began in Asia). The need is not so much for choosing one area over another but rather for looking at the two as essentially coequal.

This sense of equality is a theme that looms large in the minds of Asians themselves. Any American who travels to Asia regularly cannot help but feel the desire—and, increasingly, the demand—that Asians at all levels have for a relationship with the United States built on mutual respect and a willingness on our part to treat the nations and peoples of Asia with the degree of dignity that their cultures, resources, talents, and even numbers deserve. The old one-sidedness, the "big-brother–little-brother" attitudes that included elements of condescension and arrogance, will no longer do. Massive changes are taking place in Asia, changes that, given the extraordinary numbers of people involved (China alone, after all, now accounts for approximately 20 percent of the world population), will affect us all.

Beyond this, in several cases at least, our relations with Asia require more attention than they have received in the past because those relations not only are important, but are still fragile and unstable. Once again, due to shared cultural and historical traditions, we have learned far better how to deal with problems that arise with our principal friends in Europe. We have also learned how to handle our affairs with smaller European nations with something close to an acceptable degree of sophistication and politeness. Such is not yet the case with our dealings with the countries of Asia. Our commercial and diplomatic efforts all too often are marred by sudden lurches and failures in communication that can, on occasion, come close to spelling disaster. Certainly our treatment of Japan speaks to this point. On several issues of key importance to the Japanese over the past decade, we have taken steps of great moment, only bothering to inform the Japanese, our most important friends in Asia, after the fact—the great "Nixon shock" surrounding his dramatic and unexpected move to open relations with the People's Republic of China without keeping Japan reasonably informed, for example, and, more recently the failure of the Reagan Administration to consult with the Japanese government before lifting the grain embargo against the USSR, established in retaliation for the Soviet invasion of Afghanistan, and with strong pressure on Japan to join in the embargo action.

We have not yet, in other words, placed our relations with the nations of Asia on the kind of institutionalized base that we have European nations. This absence of institutionalization naturally leaves our dealings in Asia more prone to disruption, with misunderstanding ever a more clear and present danger.

The causes are not, to be sure, all on one side (ours) alone. Mistakes can be made on either shore and frequently are. The opening of more workable, more efficient channels of communication is a task with ample scope for contributions from any interested quarter. But given the preponderant overall role the United States plays in the pan-Pacific equation, the challenge to us is unquestionably the greater.

This is not yet the place at which to outline specific steps that might be taken either here or by Asian friends (and adversaries, should they so desire) to improve joint levels of understanding and ease points of friction. Such policy recommendations will be reserved for the closing sections of this book. It is enough for the moment, to state the problem and the need, and thus we turn now to a look at what sort of knowledge (or lack of it) Americans have of Asia.

2

Our Knowledge of Asia

Most Americans, it appears, tend to place Asia and most (but not all) countries in that part of the world in a position of secondary importance compared to countries in Europe and certain other areas that command special attention, whether it be for reasons of geography, economic power, military muscle, or the like. But what knowledge do we as a people have of Asia? How well informed are we, and how well informed do we think we are?

A series of questions in our survey yields some interesting, and not very reassuring, answers. One question, for example, simply asked respondents to rate themselves in terms of how much or how little they think they know about countries in the region—with several nations outside Asia again included for purposes of contrast.

Perceived Knowledge of Countries

I'm going to read a list of countries, some of which you may know a great deal about, some a fair amount, some not very much, and some nothing at all. As I read off the name of each country, please tell me how much you feel you know about it—a great deal, a fair amount, not very much, or nothing at all?

The responses are set forth in table 2-1.

Only in the case of Canada did more than one-quarter of the population consider that it knows "a great deal." (Canada, by the way, almost invariably ranks first on most positive indicators that rate comparable American opinion about other countries.) And only the USSR and Japan drew a similar response from at least one American in five. At the other end of the scale, a minimum of one in five admitted knowing "nothing at all" about five nations in Asia—Malaysia (where almost four in ten acknowledged no information), Indonesia, Singapore, New Zealand, and Kampuchea (referred to as Cambodia

Table 2–1
Knowledge of Countries

	A Great Deal (Percentage)	Fair Amount (Percentage)	Not Very Much (Percentage)	Nothing at All (Percentage)	Do Not Know (Percentage)
1. Canada	37	47	11	4	1
2. Japan	23	55	16	4	2
3. USSR	20	50	21	7	2
4. Israel	17	49	24	8	2
5. West Germany	15	50	27	7	1
6. Vietnam	13	46	30	9	2
7. Australia	12	47	29	10	2
8. China	10	48	33	7	2
9. Philippines	7	41	37	13	2
9. Saudi Arabia	7	41	38	12	2
11. Brazil	6	37	43	13	1
11. South Korea	6	35	45	12	2
13. India	5	39	39	15	2
13. New Zealand	5	30	41	21	3
13. Cambodia	5	26	47	20	2
13. Taiwan	5	33	44	15	3
17. North Korea	4	28	51	15	2
17. Thailand	4	25	50	19	2
19. Singapore	2	22	47	26	3
19. Nigeria	2	15	50	30	3
21. Indonesia	1	14	52	30	3
21. Malaysia	1	10	47	39	3

in the survey questionnaire). The only non-Asian country on our list about which ignorance of this extreme was expressed is Nigeria.

Among various demographic groups of Americans, a number of variations were expressed. Those who claimed to be better informed than the national norm about most of the countries listed (or, at the other end of the scale, less badly informed) included persons who exhibit high interest in international affairs and, to a lesser degree, the college educated. The more affluent (persons with annual incomes in excess of $25,000) and persons in the professional and business category also quite frequently stated higher levels of awareness than did Americans in other income brackets or occupations. Individuals with only grade-school educations and black Americans were more inclined than the national average to say they know "nothing at all," have no opinion, or were markedly below the average where knowing "a great deal" is concerned. Neither sex, age, nor region of the country where one lives played much of a role as far as stated levels of knowledge were concerned.

Sources of Information

Where do we get our information about Asia? What are the principal sources from which Americans form their impressions of that part of the world? In this survey and in two earlier (1978) Potomac studies, questions were posed that sought to shed some light on this topic:

Of the following, which are your main sources of awareness about Japan, and which are your main sources of awareness about South Korea? Please pick the one or two most important to you.

	Japan (Percent)	South Korea (Percent)
	(1978 data)	
Television and radio	65	65
Newspapers, magazines, and books	53	50
Purchase and use of Japanese (South Korean) goods	18	5
Personal contacts with Japanese (South Koreans)	9	3
Movies	4	—
Do not know	6	7

In the 1978 studies, the media, other than movies, were the most influential sources of information. Television and radio were particularly important sources of information about Japan to people with either a high school or grade-school education. Reading materials were especially important for the college educated for information about both Japan and Korea (68 percent in the case of Japan and 64 percent for Korea). Westerners cited personal contacts as an important source of awareness substantially more often than did people living elsewhere in the United States, although the numbers here were still small compared to the dominance of the electronic and print media.

For the 1980 survey, the list of sources was somewhat expanded:

I am going to read you some sources from which you may have learned about Asia. As I read each one, please tell me how much of your overall knowledge of Asia came from that particular source—a great deal, a fair amount, not very much, or none at all?

Persons "very interested" in international affairs gave substantially higher importance than the average to television news, novels, and literature, knowing Asians, school education, and purchase of goods made in Asia (see table 2-2). The college educated pointed to knowing Asians and classroom education in numbers above the norm; education was also mentioned with above-average frequency by those in the eighteen- to twenty-four-year-old age group. (On the basis of past survey evidence, newspapers and magazines, not included in this list, would have ranked in second place, after television news programs.)

It is somewhat encouraging to note that the three groups that cited classroom education as a source of knowledge and awareness more frequently than the norm are those very people for whom such training is likely to have had the greatest impact—because it is still relatively fresh in their memories (eighteen to twenty-four year olds), because they had more of it (the college educated), or, finally, because of their higher attention level to world affairs, probably

Table 2-2
Sources of Knowledge of Asia

	Great Deal (Percentage)	Fair Amount (Percentage)	Not Very Much (Percentage)	None at All (Percentage)	Do Not Know (Percentage)
Television news programs	33	39	21	6	1
Television programs (for example, special and situation comedies such as M*A*S*H	15	31	35	18	1
School and classroom education	13	33	28	25	1
Radio	9	35	34	21	1
Novels and literature	9	26	38	26	1
Purchase and use of goods made in Asia	7	27	40	25	1
Cultural events seen in this country	7	24	36	32	1
Have visited Asia	7	2	3	84	4
Knows Asians	6	13	22	57	2
Movies	3	16	47	33	1

reflecting more schooling in international events than the average (those "very interested" in international affairs).

On the other hand, it is also important to note that even among these groups classroom education was mentioned as providing "a great deal" of knowledge about Asia by fewer than three Americans in ten—27, 23, and 28 percent, respectively. And in each case one in ten (12, 11, and 10 percent, respectively) said that the classroom gave them "none at all" of their awareness of Asia. For nonwhites, grade schoolers, and persons with annual incomes under $10,000, the proportions in which school contributed nothing rose sharply, to over one-third to nearly one-half (36, 49, and 35 percent, respectively).

These numbers clearly attest to the inadequacy of training and instruction given in our educational system about Asia and its peoples, a situation that will become increasingly evident in the pages ahead. Much remains to be done.

One's place of residence in one or another of the major regions of the country (East, Midwest, South, and West for purposes of this analysis) had, comparatively, only minimal effect on how individuals rated their knowledge levels. The relative lack of influence of geographic location on attitudes, especially in the field of foreign affairs and international relations, has become increasingly apparent in a wide variety of surveys and studies undertaken in recent years. Much of this may be attributable to the simple reality, affirmed by what we have just seen, that most of us get most of our news and general information from the public media—television, newspapers, radio, and the like. And much, indeed most, of the international news carried by these institutions is filtered through a limited number of sources: the major television networks and national news services, two or three newspaper news syndicates, and a handful of national news journals. This in turn means that national and international news reporting has assumed a considerable homogeneity—thereby inevitably diminishing, if not eradicating, traditional differences in views that once depended heavily on the part of the country in which one lived. "That's the way it is," we were told (and readily accepted) for years by Walter Cronkite, and it truly became the way it is.

Asians as Neighbors

With 19 percent of the respondents saying that knowing Asians had been the source of at least a fair amount of their knowledge of Asia, it is appropriate to touch for a moment on the surge of immigration into the United States of peoples from Asia. According to reports from the Immigration and Naturalization Service, some 1.5 million Asians were legally admitted into this country between October 1, 1970, and September 30, 1980. This substantial flow, representing a sharp increase from the past, resulted from changes in the immigration laws that ended discriminatory quotas in 1968, quotas that had been in effect for over four decades under limitations set in place by the Quota Act of 1924.

Particularly large numbers of new arrivals from Asia represent five nationalities: Chinese, Japanese, Koreans, Filipinos, and Vietnamese. Census data from 1980, released by the Bureau of the Census, show that people of these nationalities now total almost 3 million, with their numbers surging in the last decade.[1]

	1970	1980	Percentage Change
Chinese	435,062	806,027	85
Filipino	343,060	774,640	126
Japanese	591,290	700,747	19
Korean	69,130	354,529	413
Vietnam	n/a	262,000	n/a

The Japanese, who were the largest Asian group in 1970, have slipped to third place, as their numbers have increased proportionately more slowly than any of the others. While Chinese have now moved into the lead, the most spectacular growth has been in the Korean population, which more than quadrupled in the last decade.

One result of this influx has been the growth of strong new ethnic communities, especially in California but in other parts of the country as well, that stand on their own, separate from the traditional "Chinatowns." Entire clusters of Korean shops, stores, grocery markets, pharmacies, and restaurants, for example, can be found in the metropolitan areas (New York, Chicago, Washington, D.C., Los Angeles, and elsewhere) and not just in the major West Coast cities.

Given this very noticeable increase in the number of Asians in the United States—an increase that may be expected to continue in the years ahead—it is interesting to note that almost one-third of the people interviewed in our survey said that there had been an increase in the number of Asians living in their community:

In recent years relatively large numbers of people from Asia have been migrating to the United States. Has there been an increase in the number of Asian people living in your community recently?

Yes	29 percent
No	70 percent
Do not know	1 percent

The college educated, members of the professional and business community, individuals with annual incomes in excess of $25,000, those very interested in international affairs, and Westerners cited an increase in the number of Asians in their area in markedly higher numbers than the average (40, 44, 39, 41, and 44 percent, respectively). Among blacks, 19 percent said they had noted an increase, whereas 80 percent said they had not.

When the responses to all the questions in our survey were cross-tabulated according to whether people said there had been an increase in the number of Asians living in their community or not, the results at first suggest that the effect of increased exposure is frequently positive, sometimes very much so. Responses to specific-knowledge questions by those who said "yes, there has been an increase in the number of Asians in the area where I live" were correct more often than for the national norm. Overall views on levels of liking Asian countries and attitudes on standard of living and political stability (to be discussed shortly) were frequently more positive.

The correlation, however, is not as clear as it initially appears. As noted previously, among those more prone than average to see an increase in the number of Asians in their community are the college educated, whose views coincide with the opinions described in the preceding paragraph. Upon further analysis, it turned out that level of education, not an increase in numbers of Asians as neighbors, was the key controlling factor. This in itself, to be sure, has direct implications for future efforts to improve the understanding Americans have of Asia and Asians, reinforcing the potential impact of schooling on our perceptions.

Knowledge of Some Specifics

The ratings Americans gave themselves on their presumed knowledge about Asian countries are not overly impressive (although one can only conjecture that the picture would not be much better if the focus was on some other part of the globe, with the possible exception of Europe). How does this overall sketchy knowledge stand up against a brief information test?

A battery of fairly basic (although not always elementary) true-false questions uncovered several clear misconceptions, in some cases carrying overtones either benefiting or harming the country involved inaccurately. Table 2–3 presents the questions and responses, with the correct answers indicated.

At least three Americans in four were correctly informed that Japan is not a key petroleum supplier to the United States, that we have major military installations in the Philippines, and that China's government is communist. But clear majorities were wide of the mark concerning the level of our trade with China (which has, of course, been growing rapidly, but which was still far from the top-15 level at the time the survey was carried out in July of 1980); Indonesia's role as a supplier of oil and petroleum products to the United States (although the totals are far outshadowed by imports from Saudi Arabia, and Nigeria, for example, Indonesia is our sixth-

Table 2–3
Knowledge of Specifics

	True (Percentage)	False (Percentage)	Do Not Know (Percentage)
1. Japan is a major supplier of oil and petroleum products imported into the United States.	8	90*	2
2. The United States has major naval and air bases in the Philippines.	81*	16	3
3. China is one of the United States' fifteen largest trading partners.	58	38*	3
4. Indonesia is a major supplier of oil and petroleum products imported into the United States.	21*	74	5
5. The Philippines was once a colony of the United States.	60*	35	5
6. The United States provides major economic assistance and aid to South Korea.	81	15*	4
7. Australia is a major supplier of beef imported into the United States.	56*	40	4
8. The government of Mainland China is not communist.	20	76*	4

*Correct answer.

largest foreign supplier); and South Korea's position as an alleged aid recipient from the United States (South Korea no longer receives any direct economic aid from us). More than one American in three did not know that the Philippines was once a U.S. colony or that Australia is a prime source of imported beef. (It is, in fact, the largest such supplier, accounting for over 50 percent of the total. Australian range-fed beef is particularly prized for its flavor in hamburgers. This is a factor that, if known by more Americans, might increase the high regard we already have for the land down under—the controversy of mid-1981 concerning the mixing in of kangaroo meat notwithstanding.)

In this regard, it is tempting to speculate that, in some instances at least, the information or misinformation of the majority bears a direct correlation with the positive or negative views that Americans hold about the country involved. The Philippines, which ranks fairly well up the like/dislike list among Asian countries, probably benefits from the knowledge correctly shared by most Americans that we continue to have vitally important military bases there (at Clark Field and Subic Bay), as well as feelings of identity because of that country's former colonial links to us. South Korea's image is only moderately good, at best, in this study (as well as in the earlier Potomac reports already cited) and is undoubtedly hurt by (among other things) the false impression that it is still a major aid recipient. Foreign aid is one of the least popular of all federal expenditures among the American people; in 1976, for example, we found that in a list of twenty-four U.S. government-spending programs, "furnishing economic aid and loans to less-developed countries" and "providing military aid to some of our allies" ranked twenty-third and twenty-fourth, respectively, in popularity among Americans! Indonesia might well rate better if Americans were aware of its substantial role as a supplier of oil and petroleum products to the United States. And the ongoing China euphoria is bound to be augmented by the impression, quite in error at the time the survey was conducted, that China was one of our leading fifteen trading partners.

It is particularly startling and disturbing to find that the college educated did not do much better than the nation as a whole on those questions where misinformation was greatest: those with college training were wrong in percentages *larger* than the norm concerning economic aid to South Korea, imports of oil from Indonesia, and (marginally so) beef supplies from Australia, and wrong by a majority proportion on the level of U.S.-China trade. This same group was not much better informed than the average concerning the former colonial status of the Philippines, something also true of those very interested in international affairs. The eighteen to twenty-four year olds, in keeping with their higher levels of favorable attitudes toward China noted in chapter 1, were especially misled on the size of our trade with China: more than three in four believed that China was one of our top fifteen trading partners.

Knowledge of Asian Governmental Systems

The considerable imprecision and uncertainty demonstrated by responses to these factual queries carried forward to identification of the type of government holding sway in the countries of Asia. In this case, the individuals being interviewed were given a card, with countries listed on the side and a choice of type of government along the top—communist, military-authoritarian, civilian-authoritarian, mixed military-civilian authoritarian, and democratic. They were asked:

> As you know, different types of governments are found in various countries. I want you to check off the answer that comes closest to describing your own impression of the kind of government in each of several countries. Look at the top of each column for the description of each type of government, then place an X in the box that best describes each country. [Questionnaire and pencil are given to respondent.]

The results are shown in table 2–4.

This is, admittedly, a complicated and difficult question, calling for relatively sophisticated knowledge about governing systems in countries that many Americans freely acknowledge they know little or nothing about. And the characterizations of the form of government are not always clear in every case, opening the way to some legitimate confusion.

Be that as it may, it still comes as further corroboration of the generally fuzzy state of many Americans' awareness of Asia that less than one-third (32 percent) called Japan democratic, while only relatively slim majorities applied this label to Australia and New Zealand (62 and 55 percent, respectively). Furthermore, at least one American in ten stated that the governments of three strongly anticommunist

Table 2–4
Type of Government
(percent mentions, first and second choice)

1.	Australia	Democratic (62); civilian authoritarian (18)
2.	Cambodia	Communist (34); military authoritarian (32)
3.	China	Communist (60); military authoritarian (15)
4.	Indonesia	Military authoritarian (27); mixed military-civilian authoritarian (27)
5.	Japan	Democratic (32); mixed military-civilian authoritarian (23)
6.	Malaysia	Mixed military-civilian authoritarian (24); military authoritarian (23)
7.	New Zealand	Democratic (55); civilian authoritarian (19)
8.	North Korea	Communist (58); military authoritarian (22)
9.	Philippines	Civilian authoritarian (25); mixed military-civilian authoritarian (23); democratic (23)
10.	Singapore	Civilian authoritarian (25); mixed military-civilian authoritarian (22)
11.	South Korea	Military authoritarian (38); mixed military-civilian authoritarian (22)
12.	USSR	Communist (86); military authoritarian (5)
13.	Taiwan	Mixed military-civilian authoritarian (24); military authoritarian (22)
14.	Thailand	Military authoritarian (27); mixed military-civilian authoritarian (24)
15.	Vietnam	Communist (54); military authoritarian (22)

Asian nations—Singapore, South Korea, and Thailand—were, in fact, communist (10, 15, and 12 percent, respectively)!

The picture that emerges from all these responses is disquieting. While it may be perfectly true that Americans' awareness of other parts of the world is not much better that their awareness of Asia, that only adds to the extent of the problem. Misinformation abounds, lack of knowledge is readily admitted. Even the better educated and those who take a special interest in international affairs occasionally show shocking gaps in their information levels.

Notes

1. See *New York Times,* June 30, 1981.

2. See Watts and Free, *State of the Nation III* (Lexington, Mass.: Lexington Books, D.C. Heath, 1978), pp. 61–62 and 161–164.

3 Stereotypes of Asia: Countries and Peoples

It is only natural for the human mind to work out a set of stereotypes in which to classify other peoples and other lands. We do it for ourselves all the time: the "big spender" from Texas is contrasted with the closed-mouthed and tight-fisted New Englander, the gracious and polite Southerner with the pushy and aggressive New Yorker. Little matter whether these images are correct in all cases—obviously, they are not. What does matter is that many of us do carry them around in our heads, and we apply them unwittingly in judgments we make and basic attitudes we form.

What happens when Americans turn their eyes, ears, and minds across the Pacific? What are some of the stereotypes that underlie their thinking and come to the fore when Asia is mentioned or when they read or hear about events in one Asian country or another? Are different countries seen differently, either as friend or foe, advanced or backward? Do Americans differentiate among various Asian peoples, or are Asians seen as if through a special lens that makes them all look alike—shades of the "yellow peril"?

Since such images are so important and shape responses to given situations so fundamentally, we decided to include in our testing of American opinion an extensive probing of various stereotypes, starting with Asia in general, then moving to a few selected countries in the region, and finally assessing views on the people in most of those countries.

Asia in General

For Asia in general, we selected a set of fifteen adjectives or phrases that might be applied to the region and asked the respondents to pick out those that came closest to their own overall impressions. Drawing up such a list is, by its very nature, highly arbitrary. The reader may have preferred that some on our roster be omitted and others added. No such selection is perfect, but the attempt was consciously made to provide a range of choice that would allow a reasonably clear and informative picture to emerge.

With this in mind, we asked:

> On this card are a number of adjectives or phrases that might be used to describe your general impression of various countries. First, when you think of countries in Asia, please tell me which of the words or phrases on this card come closest to expressing your impression of Asian countries. Just mention the two or three that come immediately to mind.

The responses, in descending order of the number of times each was mentioned, are set forth in table 3–1.

Four characterizations dominated the responses, being cited by some four in ten or more—and none of them were among the more positive words or phrases offered. "Crowded; too many people," "underdeveloped," "political unrest," and "dirty; poor sanitation." The other expressions that fitted best the thinking of Americans, enough so that they were mentioned in double-digit proportions, included "jungles," "temples," and "aggressive; warlike." The remaining suggested labels were picked out by less

Table 3–1
Stereotypes: Asia in General

	Percentage Mention All Adults
1. Crowded; too many people	61
2. Underdeveloped	49
3. Political unrest	43
4. Dirty; poor sanitation	38
5. Jungles	14
5. Temples	14
7. Aggressive; warlike	13
8. Industrialized	8
9. Much crime; unsafe	6
10. Peace loving	4
10. Modern	4
12. Well educated	3
12. Well dressed	3
14. High-quality roads, railroads, airlines, and so on	2
14. Many automobiles	2
Do not know/no answer	5

than one in ten—and these were generally the most positive and flattering portrayals.

This rather negative overall assessment and stereotyped image of Asia was held even more strongly by the college educated, members of the professional and business community, the more affluent, and those who showed themselves to be very interested in international affairs, all of whom mentioned in numbers significantly above the national average the first three items. Those, in other words, who by nature of their socioeconomic status are more likely to be closer to the sources of power in the United States are especially prone to see Asia as a whole in terms of overpopulation, economic backwardness, and political instability.

This is not to say that these characteristics are necessarily inaccurate or unfairly prejudicial. The fact is, of course, that overcrowding is a most serious problem for most countries in Asia, with even Japan, the most highly industrialized nation in the region, suffering from a severe housing shortage. Political unrest has been a continuing problem in several countries, with strong opposition groups or major political upheavals emerging in China, the Philippines, and South Korea, for example. And economic backwardness remains a central issue in China, with current efforts to stir development after years of stagnation causing sharp divisions within the Chinese Communist Party leadership.

But along with these problem areas, on which Americans tend to focus, there have been some extraordinary advances in many Asian nations, with the emergence of Japan as a global economic superpower the most obvious and the one that attracts the most attention. Have we responded to individual changes with any degree of discrimination? Do Americans apply different labels to different countries within the region, or does the stereotype for Asia as a whole hold for its component parts?

Selected Countries in Asia

In fact, Americans draw sharply contrasting sketches of various Asian nations. In looking at these images as they emerged from responses to the following question, one can argue that the contrasting views are, for the most part, a reasonably direct reflection of the nature of reporting of developments in each of the countries by

American newspapers, television, radio, and other public-information sources. That the images are not fully in keeping with current realities throughout is a measure of the weaknesses in that reporting as well as the traditional picture of these countries carried in standard textbooks.

> Let's think now just about a few countries in particular. As I read off the names of certain nations, please tell me which of the adjectives or phrases come closest to describing your impression of that country. Just tell me the two or three that best fit your image of each country. (Call off the numbers, please.)

The responses are contained in table 3-2, with those stereotypical adjectives or phrases mentioned by at least 20 percent of the respondents included, listed in descending order.

China, Indonesia, the Philippines, South Korea, Thailand, and Vietnam were all viewed by Americans in terms fairly close to those of the picture of Asia in general. Thus the three phrases or words picked most often by Americans in thinking of the area as a whole—crowded, underdeveloped, and political unrest—were also mentioned by at least one respondent in five as applying to these six countries. Dirty and poor sanitation—the next characterization selected most often for the region—was picked by our cutoff of 20 percent or more for all but China; jungles—which followed for Asia—met the test for all but China and South Korea; whereas aggressive—seventh on the overall list—was chosen only for Vietnam among this group of the countries.

In varying degrees, these characterizations of the countries in question can be accepted as reasonably accurate. Overcrowding is a widespread problem, and political unrest and inadequate sanitary facilities are endemic to several of them. And Vietnam, with its invasion of Cambodia, has established its aggressiveness for all to see. (China's incursion into Vietnam in February of 1979, to "teach a lesson" to its ambitious and pugnacious neighbor, did not earn it a similar reputation; in the new pro-Chinese atmosphere that has settled on the United States, only a relatively small proportion—12 percent—equated the People's Republic with aggression.)

The blanket application of underdevelopment to all these countries, however, is surely open to question. Both China and Vietnam are beset with developmental problems, but Indonesia, Thailand, and the Philippines have made considerable strides in recent years.

Table 3–2
Stereotypes: Selected Countries

Country	Percentage of Agreeing with Stereotypes Mentioned by at Least One in Five (20 Percent)	
1. Australia	Modern	45
	Peace-loving	45
	Industrialized	31
	Well educated	26
	Well dressed	20
	Underdeveloped	20
2. China	Crowded; too many people	76
	Underdeveloped	37
	Political unrest	22
3. Indonesia	Crowded; too many people	46
	Underdeveloped	44
	Dirty; poor sanitation	32
	Political unrest	29
	Jungles	24
4. Japan	Industrialized	50
	Crowded; too many people	42
	Well educated	38
	Modern	30
	Many automobiles	23
5. Philippines	Underdeveloped	36
	Crowded; too many people	32
	Jungles	30
	Dirty; poor sanitation	26
	Political unrest	24
6. South Korea	Political unrest	47
	Underdeveloped	39
	Crowded; too many people	33
	Dirty; poor sanitation	33
7. USSR	Aggressive; warlike	57
	Industrialized	51
	Political unrest	32
	Well educated	21
8. Taiwan	Crowded; too many people	46
	Industrialized	29
	Underdeveloped	26
9. Thailand	Underdeveloped	38
	Crowded; too many people	36
	Dirty; poor sanitation	29
	Political unrest	25
	Jungles	21
10. Vietnam	Dirty; poor sanitation	44
	Political unrest	43
	Underdeveloped	38
	Jungles	34
	Crowded; too many people	32
	Aggressive; warlike	31

South Korea has emerged as one of the economic success stories of the region and, indeed, of the globe, with growth rates that have made it a recognized figure in international markets (and the United States' thirteenth largest trading partner); yet a scant 6 percent referred to industrialization in connection with this country.

Taiwan, on the other hand, represented a slight break from the norm. A substantial proportion saw it as industrialized, while an almost equal number thought of it as underdeveloped. The influx into the American marketplace of products made in Taiwan apparently has begun to register on the American people and has given Taiwan a slightly special cachet here. It should be noted that the leading stereotype for the region—overpopulation—was also picked first for Taiwan.

The USSR is clearly another special case. Seen first and foremost as both aggressive and industrialized, the USSR was the only country in the region that presented a distinctly threatening image. This obviously goes hand in hand with the substantially high levels of dislike that so many Americans had of the country. Political unrest also ranked high, as it did for most nations in the region; the Soviet authorities' continuing crackdown on activities of dissidents within the country and the banishment into internal or overseas exile of some of the most prominent, events all widely reported in the United States, have left their mark on the minds of Americans. On a more positive note, the USSR is one of only three countries on this particular list that at least one American in five thought of in terms of its people being well educated.

The other two nations that fall into this category are Japan and Australia—the two Asian nations that consistently stand near the top of the ratings given by Americans on most of the indicators we have used. Both Japan and Australia were also viewed by three in ten or more as industrialized and modern. Japan, hardly surprisingly, was the only country where the presence of many automobiles was a commonly cited factor, while Australia (like Taiwan) was seen by substantial proportions as both industrialized and underdeveloped—the latter almost certainly stemming from the images of the "outback," desert, and aborigines that are much a part of Australian literature, films, and television programming seen in the United States.

The variations in perceptions of these selected nations of Asia among population groups in the United States may hold special significance in considering targets for information or other programs.

Particularly noticeable differences are summarized in the following country-by-country listing.

Australia. The college educated and the more affluent were consistently above the norm in mentioning the more positive stereotypes. Blacks and grade schoolers mentioned the principal words or phrases in numbers well below the average, both here and in most other country ratings.

China. The college educated, Westerners, and those somewhat interested in international affairs tended to mention the key indicators more often than the national average.

Indonesia. The college educated, members of the professional and business community, the more affluent, and those very interested in foreign affairs tended to run above the norm in citing the key indicators listed for this country.

Japan. The college educated and those very interested in international affairs pointed with greater frequency to industrialization, modernization, and education.

Philippines. In this case, it was the college educated, the more affluent, and those very interested in international affairs who were usually above the norm in picking the key stereotypes.

South Korea. The college educated, the more affluent, members of the professional and business community, and the very interested were especially conscious of political unrest. All but the last also referred to underdevelopment in larger than average numbers.

USSR. Those more inclined to select industrialization included Americans eighteen to twenty-four years of age, the college educated, the more affluent, and those somewhat interested in international affairs.

Taiwan. Those in the eighteen to twenty-four year age group were more inclined to view Taiwan as underdeveloped and less inclinded to see it as industrialized than the norm. They also cited overcrowding with high frequency. On the other hand, the college educated, the more affluent, and the very interested referred to industrialization in higher than average proportions.

Thailand. The college educated, members of the professional and business community, the more affluent, and the very interested were regularly higher than the norm in their perceptions of political unrest and lack of economic development.

Vietnam. These same themes—political unrest and underdevelopment—were also strongly on the minds of the college educated, the more affluent, and those very interested in international affairs.

As was the case for stereotypes of Asia as a whole, so again in this series of specific countries: the better educated, the more affluent, members of the business and professional community, and those more interested in international affairs tended to gravitate toward the more frequently cited words or phrases than did the populace at large. In essence, the sharpening of views that seems to go with improved education and economic or professional position more often than not gains expression in an increased level of mentioning the more prevalent stereotypes—whether they be positive or negative, favorable or unfavorable, as far as the perception of the individual country is concerned.

While this is altogether understandable and even to be expected, it also underlines once again the tremendous responsibility placed on our educational system and the major sources of public information. To the extent they are accurate and fair in what they dispense, then increased levels of knowledge and interest tend to result in better and more sophisticated awareness. But where the classrooms and the media place undue emphasis on a limited part of the whole concerning a given country—China's emergence onto the world's economy after an extended period of isolation, for example, or South Korea's unstable and authoritarian image—the result can be an evident exaggeration of strengths (as here in the case of China, whose economic problems remain staggering) and weaknesses (where, in the situation of Korea, remarkable economic advances are almost totally overlooked due to a preoccupation with that country's political problems, real though they may be).

It is not only the responsibility of schools, colleges, television, and other information outlets to add to our national store of understanding and awareness of Asia, its lands, and its peoples but leadership at all levels on both sides of the Pacific must play a role as well. Indeed, their contribution may be the most important of all since it can do so much to set the tone for many other activities.

Peoples of Selected Asian Countries

The basic stereotypes of Asia as a whole and of several countries in the region have been marked, one can argue, by a good deal of reasonably fair and accurate interpretations, accompanied by some very unfair and inaccurate biases and examples of fundamental factual misinformation. What about perceptions of the people themselves in some of these countries? Once again, do Americans differentiate, or are Asians seen as a relatively homogeneous grouping, with little in the way of personality, cultural, and social distinctiveness from one land to another?

For peoples of eight countries, at least, Americans hold some sharply contrasting views, as responses to another question in our survey made clear:

> I am going to hand you this part of the questionnaire to make it easier for you to answer the following questions. For each of the questions, you will see some pairs of words or phrases that, in general, could be used to describe the people of certain countries. I want you to look at each pair of words and check the one that comes closest to your impression of the people of the country mentioned. For example, if you think the people of a country are hard-working you would put an X in the box beside that word; if you feel the people are lazy, you would put an X beside that word. For each pair of words, put only one X. Be sure to give an answer for each set of words.

For each of the countries rated, respondents were asked to choose between the following word pairs:

Hard-working-lazy
Imitative-creative
Peaceful-warlike
Humble-arrogant
Treacherous-loyal
Straightforward-deceitful
Individualistic-group oriented
Competitive-noncompetitive
Undisciplined-disciplined

Responses for each country are set forth in table 3–3, with the word of each pair that was chosen by the majority or plurality listed in the first column.

As in the case of adjectives or descriptive phrases chosen to test comparative attitudes toward Asia as a whole or individual countries in the region, so too is this set of contrasting characteristics open to secondguessing. Whatever the reader's reactions may be to the pairs selected, the intent was pure—to try to come up with a grouping that would reveal something meaningful about the biases, prejudices, and assorted other reactions that Americans have about some of the peoples of Asia. The results, I believe, are instructive.

If we begin with what might be accepted as standard American values, it seems fair to say that the preferred personality traits would include the following: hard-working, creative, peaceful, humble, loyal, straightforward, competitive, disciplined, and (presumably, but open to discussion) individualistic.

If this assessment is accepted as valid, then the peoples of two countries conform most nearly to the ideal, with the choice between individualistic and group oriented being the point of contention. As might be expected from earlier ratings of countries in the region, the two peoples involved are *Australians* (seen as individualistic) and *Japanese* (considered group oriented, as was the case for all other nationalities included in this list). For the most part, the margins for Australians and Japanese in favor of each characteristic that we would expect Americans to prefer ran at least three to one and sometimes substantially higher (forty-seven to one, for example, in the case of Japanese as hard-working versus lazy!).

Taking Japanese and Australians as a hypothetical ideal stereotype (and with no personal preference implied or intended), it is interesting to see how Americans viewed other Asians in comparison, and to speculate on some of the reasons why they made the selections they did.

The generally positive ratings given both Japan and Australia in some of our earlier discussion (with more of the same to come as we consider other measures of approval or respect) surely stem in part from the fact that Americans evidently see in Japanese and Australians many of the attributes they find most compatible with their own preferences. To the extent that other peoples do not conform to such preferences, they are likely to be less in favor with the American people.

Table 3–3
Percentage Agreeing with Stereotypes: People of Selected Countries

Australia

Hard-working	87	Lazy	6	Do not know	7
Creative	67	Imitative	23		10
Peaceful	89	Warlike	3		8
Humble	66	Arrogant	23		11
Loyal	86	Treacherous	5		9
Straightforward	86	Deceitful	4		10
Individualistic	70	Group oriented	19		11
Competitive	69	Noncompetitive	20		11
Disciplined	81	Undisciplined	10		9

China

Hard-working	91	Lazy	5		4
Creative	55	Imitative	39		6
Peaceful	55	Warlike	39		6
Humble	63	Arrogant	31		6
Loyal	60	Treacherous	33		7
Straightforward	55	Deceitful	37		8
Group oriented	80	Individualistic	14		6
Competitive	63	Noncompetitive	31		6
Disciplined	83	Undisciplined	11		6

Japan

Hard-working	95	Lazy	2		3
Creative	72	Imitative	24		4
Peaceful	69	Warlike	25		6
Humble	66	Arrogant	29		5
Loyal	70	Treacherous	23		7
Straightforward	64	Deceitful	28		8
Group oriented	63	Individualistic	32		5
Competitive	86	Noncompetitive	10		4
Disciplined	87	Undisciplined	8		5

Philippines

Hard-working	70	Lazy	21		9
Creative	45	Imitative	43		12
Peaceful	79	Warlike	11		10
Humble	72	Arrogant	16		12
Loyal	75	Treacherous	14		11
Straightforward	69	Deceitful	17		14
Group oriented	64	Individualistic	24		12
Competitive	44	Noncompetitive	44		12
Disciplined	60	Undisciplined	27		13

South Korea

Hard-working	70	Lazy	23		7
Imitative	60	Creative	30		10
Peaceful	50	Warlike	41		9
Humble	53	Arrogant	37		10
Loyal	51	Treacherous	39		10

Table 3–3 continued

South Korea (continued)					
Straightforward	46	Deceitful	43	Do not know	11
Group oriented	71	Individualistic	19		10
Competitive	46	Noncompetitive	44		10
Disciplined	54	Undisciplined	38		8
USSR					
Hard-working	87	Lazy	8		5
Imitative	54	Creative	39		7
Warlike	72	Peaceful	22		6
Arrogant	69	Humble	24		7
Treacherous	58	Loyal	36		6
Deceitful	67	Straightforward	26		7
Group oriented	74	Individualistic	20		6
Competitive	68	Noncompetitive	25		7
Disciplined	81	Undisciplined	13		6
Taiwan					
Hard-working	79	Lazy	10		11
Creative	45	Imitative	43		12
Peaceful	68	Warlike	18		14
Humble	65	Arrogant	20		15
Loyal	68	Treacherous	18		14
Straightforward	65	Deceitful	19		16
Group oriented	67	Individualistic	20		13
Competitive	60	Noncompetitive	26		14
Disciplined	66	Undisciplined	21		13
Vietnam					
Hard-working	56	Lazy	36		8
Imitative	65	Creative	24		11
Warlike	66	Peaceful	25		9
Arrogant	49	Humble	40		11
Treacherous	60	Loyal	29		11
Deceitful	65	Straightforward	23		12
Group oriented	79	Individualistic	12		9
Noncompetitive	52	Competitive	37		11
Undisciplined	52	Disciplined	39		9

China. While characteristics attributed to the Chinese stayed rather close to the favored norm, at least one-third of the respondents viewed Chinese as imitative, warlike, treacherous, or deceitful. Thus, although other features (overcrowding, underdevelopment, and political unrest, for example) ran ahead of aggressiveness as a characteristic for China as a *nation,* a substantial minority did view the *people* as warlike, when given an either/or choice to make; memories of the Korean War have not disappeared altogether. Nor have some of the stereotypes prevalent in some literature on China, and the anti-

Chinese sentiments that flourished during the great influx of Chinese immigrants around the turn of the century ("cheap coolie labor" and "no dogs or Chinese allowed" come to mind).

This reservoir of negative feelings and some ill-will in the minds of a considerable proportion of Americans should not be completely dropped from sight in the midst of the current pro-Chinese euphoria. National moods can change dramatically, as indeed the shift already noted concerning China demonstrates so effectively. Given an unpredictable set of future circumstances, the base for a swing away from the present highly favorable trend does exist.

Philippines. As with the Chinese, Filipinos were seen in terms close to the hypothetical national norm. Citations of imitative and noncompetitive were high, however, essentially tied with their opposites. The positive factors in the minds of Americans (awareness of security ties exemplified by our bases in the Philippines and memories of a past colonial link-up) carried over here, leading Americans generally to choose the more favored of each pair and overshadowing negative reporting on the authoritarian Marcos government and widespread discussion of human-rights issues in the country.

South Korea. By a margin of two to one, Koreans were seen as imitative, not creative. Also, mentions of warlike, arrogant, treacherous, deceitful, noncompetitive, and undisciplined were mentioned by over a third of the American people.

There are a number of factors that contribute to what has increasingly emerged in these pages as a heavily unfavorable impression of South Korea and its people among many Americans. "Koreagate," the highly publicized and long-running episode centering on charges of attempted influence buying of members of Congress and other influential figures in Washington by prominent Korean businessmen, with allegations of Korean official involvement, undoubtedly has had much to do with this poor image. So also has the continuation of political change in the country, surrounded with periods of violence and bloodshed, including the armed overthrow of one president, Syngman Rhee, and the assassination of another, Park Chunghee. Perhaps most meaningful for most Americans, however, may be the extraordinarily popular and enduring television program "M*A*S*H," an ongoing fixture of our television fare that evokes memories of a bitter war and loss of many American lives, that shows

Koreans (or at least persons in the program that depict Koreans) in positions of inferiority and servitude and that characterizes Korea as barren, backward, and poor.[1] Much of that portrayal is far outdated, but it remains the most prevalent source of information about South Korea for most Americans.

Soviet Union. Viewed more negatively than most, Russians (or "people of the Soviet Union," in the wording of the questionnaire) were labeled by clear majorities as imitative, warlike, arrogant, treacherous, and deceitful. While the USSR commands respect for its power and importance, as we saw earlier, it garners little good will either as a nation or in terms of its people—an impression only exacerbated by the Soviet invasion and attempted subjugation of Afghanistan.

Taiwan. The people of Taiwan were ranked in terms closely in line with the generally preferred list; the exception was a virtual tie between creative and imitative as a character trait. In considerable contrast with views about Chinese on the mainland, who were seen by substantial minorities (of one-third or more) as warlike, treacherous, and deceitful, those on Taiwan were assessed more positively: twenty percent or less of our respondents opted for each of these three negative attributes. Official U.S. rupture of diplomatic relations with the authorities in Taipei and recognition of the People's Republic and its government in Beijing have not meant that Americans have decided to turn their backs on their former allies.

I noted earlier the astounding shift of American opinion toward the People's Republic—from a balance of two to one negative in 1977 to something approaching three to one positive in 1980. Coupled with this, it should be stressed, has been retention of an almost equally positive feeling toward Taiwan: a preponderance of opinion that was three to one favorable in 1977 changed little in succeeding years and essentially matched attitudes toward the People's Republic at the time we tested Americans' views in 1980.

Some loyalties, it would appear, do not die quickly.

Vietnam. Vietnamese fared even worse than Russians, labeled with the less favored characteristic in almost every case: imitative, warlike, treacherous, deceitful, noncompetitive, and undisciplined were selected by majority, and arrogant by plurality, proportions. One-third of the sample called Vietnamese ''lazy.'' Negative memories of our participation in the Vietnamese debacle have not totally lost their sting, and the Vietnamese drive into Cambodia presumably has not eased lingering resentments or angers.

Readers interested in additional detail may find some items of note in the following principal differentials in attitudes among various American population groups (with contrasts mentioned being in comparison with the overall averages).

Australians were given markedly lower ratings by blacks in terms of being hard-working, creative, individualistic, and competitive, probably reflecting black skepticism and distaste for Australian immigration policies. The more affluent found Australians especially loyal and straightforward. So did those very interested in international affairs, who also viewed Australians as individualistic.

Chinese were seen by eighteen to twenty-four year olds as more creative and less humble than the average percentages indicated. The more affluent, on the other hand, by a bare majority saw Chinese as imitative—the only group to hold this view. Midwesterners were more favorable to the Chinese on several counts—and by substantial proportions in calling them humble and straightforward. The group that deviated most from the norm was the very interested, probably especially affected by the massive outpouring of news, articles, and other reports from and about China in recent years; by margins considerably above the norm they saw Chinese as creative, humble, loyal, straightforward, and noncompetitive.

Japanese were given the more negative characterization in larger than average numbers by black Americans in several instances: imitative, warlike, arrogant, treacherous, deceitful, and undisciplined— all, it should be added, still in minority proportions. The very interested were more inclined to see Japanese as straightforward and individualistic. Westerners were less inclined than average to see Japanese as peaceful, humble, and loyal, with Easterners above the norm in each case. Age, it should be noted, played no statistically significant role here; perhaps memories of World War II have been absorbed rather equally across the board and do not enter as a negative factor any more (or less) actively into the thinking of those old enough to have been directly involved than of those for whom that particular war is a textbook matter.

Filipinos were seen more often by the very interested as imitative, humble, group oriented, and noncompetitive. Westerners were generally more negative than people in other parts of the country, leaning toward the less favorable adjective in several instances—particularly arrogant and noncompetitive. The eighteen to twenty-four year olds shared the noncompetitive image.

South Koreans were more likely to be seen as peaceful and humble by the college educated. The latter characteristic also was preferred by the very interested, along with loyal, straightforward, and competitive. Blacks rated Koreans well above the norm for being hard-working and individualistic.

For Russians ("people of the Soviet Union," in the survey questionnaire), the college educated were moderately more favorable toward the terms "peaceful" (as were the very interested) and "straightforward," although still in minority proportions. By a bare majority the college educated saw Russians as loyal over treacherous.

Taiwan was viewed by the college educated in higher than average numbers as hard-working, straightforward, and disciplined. So did the very interested, who also found the people of Taiwan more competitive, individualistic, and loyal. Members of the clerical and sales force rated the Taiwanese less favorably on being competitive, creative, and humble.

Vietnamese fared better in the eyes of the very interested and Westerners than with others, with those groups readier to think of Vietnamese as hard-working, loyal, straightforward, and disciplined. Blacks shared more moderate views where loyalty and straightforwardness are concerned.

As a general statement, I think it can be asserted that the stereotypes we have seen in this chapter evince a bit more sophistication and awareness about Asia, its countries, and its peoples than the uncertain levels of knowledge demonstrated in the preceding section might have suggested. Just as before, however, many impressions were very wide of the mark, a condition that holds true when we turn to another set of images of Asia, this time more sociopolitical in nature.

Note

1. For a fuller discussion of this point, see Richard L. Sneider and William Watts, *The United States and Korea: New Directions for the '80s* (Washington, D.C.: Potomac Associates, 1980), pp. 12 ff.

4

Stereotypes of Asia: Quality of Life, Political Stability, and Human Rights

The portrait we developed in the last chapter focused on overall personality or character traits, whether for Asia as a whole, some of its member countries, or the people who inhabit them. It is time now to turn to another set of images that Americans hold of Asian nations (and some others as well), dealing first with attitudes about comparative quality of life, or standard of living, and political stability. These topics command a good deal of attention in international-affairs reporting, and as, could be expected, Americans have contrasting views about them.

Quality of Life

With overcrowding and underdevelopment as the first two thoughts that came to mind for most Americans when asked to point to their dominant impression of Asia, it is not surprising that many Asian countries are given moderate to poor ratings where standard of living is concerned. This emerges from responses to a question that used the scale technique described in chapter 1 for measuring relative levels of like and dislike:

> We would also like to know your impression of the quality of life of various countries—that is, how high or low you think the standard of living for people is. If +5 represents a country with a very high standard of living, and −5 a country whose standard of living is very low, how would you rate the standard of living in [country]?

In table 4-1, the countries are listed in rank order, starting with "very high" perceptions, that is, the percentage total of +5 and +4 ratings. What is most striking about this listing is the fact that, with only limited exceptions, the rank order is remarkably similar to that given for levels of like and dislike. Once again, Australia, Japan, and New Zealand led other Asian nations by substantial margins. The

41

Table 4–1
Standard of Living

	Very High (Percentage)	Moderately High (Percentage)	Moderately Low (Percentage)	Very Low (Percentage)	Do Not Know (Percentage)
1. Canada	70	24	1	1	4
2. Australia	47	43	3	1	6
3. West Germany	40	46	7	2	5
4. Japan	33	51	8	3	5
5. New Zealand	22	58	9	2	9
6. Israel	18	57	15	4	6
7. Brazil	14	59	15	3	9
8. Saudi Arabia	12	43	28	9	8
9. Philippines	10	57	22	4	7
10. USSR	9	40	28	18	5
11. China	8	47	29	11	5
12. Taiwan	6	48	30	9	7
13. Singapore	5	42	33	9	11
14. Thailand	4	31	41	14	10
15. South Korea	3	37	39	14	7
15. Nigeria	3	29	42	14	12
17. Indonesia	2	31	42	10	15
17. Malaysia	2	28	41	12	17
17. India	2	25	37	29	7
17. North Korea	2	21	48	20	9
17. Vietnam	2	12	41	38	7

only noteworthy changes relate to the USSR and India, and this especially if the "very high" and "moderately high" ratings are joined together. Under these circumstances the USSR moves several steps up the list, and India drops even closer to the bottom. The USSR and India, it should be noted, together with Vietnam and North Korea, dominate the "very low" standard-of-living category.

But if the rank order is similar between these two categories of measurement, the absolute levels most certainly are not. Thus for all the countries in table 4–1 below Saudi Arabia, the combined positive ratings ("very high" and "moderately high") given for quality of life are markedly below those given for like/dislike (with the exception of the USSR, just mentioned). In other words, the overall image that Americans hold of most of the Asian countries included in this attitudinal assessment is far more positive than their perception of the standard of living or quality of life in those countries: the Philippines, China, Taiwan, Singapore, Thailand, South Korea, Indonesia,

Malaysia, North Korea, and Vietnam (which follow Saudi Arabia, in that order, on the quality-of-life reading) all drop by as much as 20 percentage points or more in the totals for standard of living as compared to popularity.

That is a large falloff, indeed. Given what has been something of an American obsession with the pursuit of the "better life," this rather drab vision of life in Asia could carry with it very subtle overtones of condescension or superiority.

One other point deserves mention here. As was also true in the measurements of favorable or unfavorable feelings about these countries, for most nations in Asia the category that Americans picked most frequently when asked to rate quality of life was + 1, usually followed by − 1 and then + 2. Coming down as close to the middle as possible could be a firm judgment by some that the quality of life in country X was, in fact, just barely on the plus side. But for others it may also have been an indication of uncertainty, a reflection of belief that things in country X (about which the respondent may know little, as indicated in earlier findings) are beyond his or her knowledge, and that, on the basis of limited information, a minimum positive rating would be the safest. Such mushy and relatively unformed views are more open to influence and alteration than those held more strongly. In many cases, they probably represent an alternative to admitting that one does not know or has no opinion.

It is not easy to compare the views Americans have about the standard of living in various Asian countries with the realities in the countries themselves. Several commonly accepted indicators are set forth in table 4–2 and will allow at least some assessment of the validity of views we have examined.

When looked at in light of these indicators, it appears that Americans underrate the standard of living in several countries when compared with others on the list. Singapore, South Korea, Taiwan, and Malaysia all should stand ahead of the Philippines, China, Thailand, and Indonesia, while Singapore also surpasses the USSR in terms of per-capita income, lower infant mortality rates, and education as a percentage of public expenditure. The Philippines in particular is accorded comparatively a more favorable quality of life than these statistics suggest, most likely resulting from the good will (in Americans' eyes) associated with that country's former colonial status and the presence there of U.S. bases. China too ranks substantially higher than per-capita income—the most obvious indicator and the one more apt to be noted in general reporting on the country—would call

Table 4–2
Standard-of-Living Indicators

Country (In Order of Listing in Table 4-1)	Per-Capita Income: US$ 1979	Infant Mortality per 1,000	Population per Physician (1,000)	Education as Percent of Public Expenditure	Percentage Literate Adults
1. Canada	9,674	14	0.5	9	98
2. Australia	8,291	14	0.8	10	100
3. Japan	9,100	9	0.9	12	99
4. New Zealand	5,938	16	0.7	14	99
5. Philippines	618	65	3	14	87
6. USSR	2,085	25	0.3	20	99
7. China	253	20	1	22	95
8. Taiwan	1,600	25	2	18	82
9. Singapore	4,150	12	1	25	75
10. Thailand	599	68	8	16	82
11. South Korea	1,636	37	2	15	91
12. Indonesia	240	126	16	8	62
13. Malaysia	1,523	32	4	19	60
14. India	204	134	3	11	36
15. North Korea	380	20	1	10	95
16. Vietnam	60	62	5	—	87
United States	10,624	15	0.6	19	99

Source: Courtesy of the Co-Convenors of Williamsburg X. Reprinted with permission.

for, once again reflecting the remarkably positive image this erstwhile adversary has attained in just a few years.

Political Stability

Political unrest, it will be recalled, was the third most prominent factor selected from a list of stereotypes about Asia when Americans were asked to think in general terms about that part of the world. We have also seen, however, that this characterization was not applied uniformly to selected countries in the region. Responses to another question in our survey bring the comparative attitudes of Americans into considerably sharper focus:

> We are also interested in your impressions of the political stability of various nations. If +5 represents a nation that is very stable politically, and −5 a nation that is not at all stable politically, how would you rate [country]?

In table 4–3, the countries are listed in rank order according to "very stable" perceptions, that is, the percentage total of mentions of +4 and +5 ratings.

In terms of perceived political stability, Australia, Japan, and New Zealand were once again rated high, leading the nations of Asia, but joined for an exceptional change by the USSR. As a general rule, political stability lagged behind popularity in the overall views expressed by about all these Asian countries, with the principal exceptions being the USSR just mentioned, and, to a lesser but still notable degree, China and North Korea.

It is also worth noting that Americans viewed almost all nations in Asia as having overall a higher level of political stability than quality of life: Australia, New Zealand, and South Korea were the exceptions. For the first two, the general image of well-being slightly surpasses what is also seen as a very solid political base. For South

Table 4–3
Political Stability

	Very Stable (Percentage)	Moderately Stable (Percentage)	Moderately Unstable (Percentage)	Very Unstable (Percentage)	Do not Know (Percentage)
1. Canada	68	24	2	1	5
2. Australia	52	34	4	1	9
3. West Germany	40	41	9	3	7
4. Japan	39	46	9	1	5
5. USSR	36	27	16	16	5
6. New Zealand	32	45	7	2	14
7. China	29	49	12	4	6
8. Israel	24	47	17	6	6
9. Brazil	16	53	17	2	12
10. Philippines	15	53	18	3	11
11. Saudi Arabia	13	53	25	10	9
12. Singapore	10	50	21	3	16
12. Taiwan	10	46	27	5	12
14. North Korea	7	28	36	18	11
15. India	6	45	31	8	10
16. Thailand	5	38	35	7	15
16. South Korea	5	32	40	14	9
18. Nigeria	4	32	38	10	16
19. Indonesia	3	40	31	5	21
19. Malaysia	3	38	28	6	25
19. Vietnam	3	19	40	29	9

Korea, however, continuing internal problems, heavily reported in the United States, pushed the political-stability ratings below those for standard of living.

Thus, South Korea joined Vietnam, North Korea, and the USSR as the countries in Asia singled out most frequently as being "very unstable." The case of the USSR is an interesting one since it ranks high at both extremes. Its authoritarian, police-state image surely promotes the impression of political stability that Americans feel, but the highly publicized activities of dissidents both with the USSR and in exile fosters notions of instability. It is also quite possible that the high level of animosity felt toward the USSR, as exemplified in the preponderantly negative attitudes it generates in the like/dislike scale, leads a considerable number of Americans to take an anti-USSR stance on almost any topic.

To a very large degree, of course, reporting of events overseas does focus on issues of policy, politics, and, increasingly, economics. In turn, these topics tend to be treated within the framework of the contribution they make to, or take away from, regional and global stability. It is interesting to note, then, that those Americans who follow international affairs most closely—that is, those most inclined to read a variety of journals and magazines that devote major attention to world events—have a more positive picture of the relative political stability of a number of Asian countries. Some striking examples follow.

Political Stability
(Very stable, +4 and +5)

	Total Adult Population (Percent)	Those "Very Interested" in International Affairs (Percent)	Change in Percent
Australia	52	70	+ 18
Japan	39	56	+ 17
USSR	36	45	+ 9
New Zealand	32	58	+ 26
China	28	45	+ 17
Taiwan	10	22	+ 12
North Korea	7	20	+ 13

The biggest surprise on this list to some would probably be North Korea, where the question of leadership succession that will be called for by the eventual passing from the scene of the durable Kim Il-sung is far from clear. As in the case of the USSR, however, the image of North Korea as a harsh and thoroughly entrenched dictatorship—the terms in which it is frequently portrayed—lends it an air of stability that is sharpened for those more interested in world events. One might also raise an eyebrow at the markedly more favorable view held by these individuals about China, where considerable uncertainty about long-term trends has been a staple of the political scene, a condition that was far from resolved at the time our survey was conducted. It almost appears that there has been a suspension of critical faculties by many Americans where China is concerned.

Heightened interest in international affairs can also work the other way and accentuate feelings about political *instability* in certain countries. This proved to be the case for both South Korea and Vietnam:

Political Stability
(Very Unstable, − 4 and − 5)

Country	Total Adult Population (Percent)	Those "Very Interested" in International Affairs (Percent)	Change in Percent
South Korea	14	30	+ 16
Vietnam	29	37	+ 8

Reasons for this increased sense of political instability in South Korea have already been discussed. Vietnam's image has been severely affected not only by continuing reports of factionalism and political infighting within the country but especially by the flight and/or expulsion of many individuals and families who either wanted to leave or were considered undesirable by the authorities there—the drama and anguish of the "boat people," which lent Vietnam an aura of cruelty combined with lack of control and inability to assimilate the conquered peoples of the South. And the continuing Vietnam-China hostility, ever fraught with the possibility of renewed border conflict, could easily enhance perceptions among Americans of instability for the Vietnamese leadership.

Human Rights

One of the principal enunciated foreign-policy objectives under President Carter and his administration was the promotion of human rights, a goal accorded lesser emphasis by his successor. Given the prominence this topic has received and the debate that surrounded the pursuit of human rights as a policy tool, we asked Americans how they viewed the status of human rights in certain Asian countries:

> Now I am going to ask you specifically your impression of the situation in various countries today as it concerns the human-rights issue, that is, the degree to which the rights and liberties of their individual citizens are protected. What is your impression about the situation in [country] concerning human rights—very favorable, somewhat favorable, somewhat unfavorable, or very unfavorable?

Tables 4-4 and 4-5 reinforce what has become by now a very familiar pattern—Australia and Japan given substantially the most positive ratings and Australia accorded a commanding lead by Americans who see the human-rights situation there as "very favorable" (better than two to one over Japan).

Somewhat surprisingly, perhaps, in view of enduring political problems and the publicity and news coverage (rather limited, to be sure) given the treatment of political opponents and dissidents in the

Table 4-4
Human Rights: Selected Countries

	Very Favorable (Percentage)	Somewhat Favorable (Percentage)	Somewhat Unfavorable (Percentage)	Very Unfavorable (Percentage)	Do Not Know (Percentage)
1. Australia	57	31	5	1	6
2. Japan	27	47	14	4	8
3. Philippines	8	49	25	8	10
4. Taiwan	7	35	31	10	17
5. China	4	27	35	25	9
6. South Korea	2	22	41	22	13
7. USSR	2	9	25	59	5
8. Vietnam	1	7	24	63	5

Table 4–5
Human Rights: Positive/Negative Balance

	All Adults (Percentage)	Those Very Interested in International Affairs (Percentage)
1. Australia	88– 6	96– 4
2. Japan	74–18	79–18
3. Philippines	57–33	45–54
4. Taiwan	42–41	44–50
5. China	31–60	24–72
6. South Korea	24–63	16–78
7. USSR	11–84	14–85
8. Vietnam	8–87	2–98

Philippines, that country ranked relatively well, with a favorable/unfavorable balance of close to two to one among all adult Americans. We see here yet another reflection, noted earlier, of the good will Americans hold toward the Philippines, given substance by their awareness of past colonial ties and present security links. Critics of the government of President Ferdinand Marcos would certainly argue that the situation concerning human rights would not permit an assessment so far ahead of conditions in South Korea, for example, where developments had, prior to President Reagan's inauguration, received far more critical attention from U.S. government sources and the American media.

The generally very positive feelings about China that we have seen thus far did not hold firm on the human-rights question, with China lagging well behind Taiwan. This shift from a pattern that has become fairly standard makes clear that the tendency to let one's critical faculties be dulled when thinking about China does not necessarily obtain in all cases.

Another standard pattern most certainly *does* remain in force when human rights are at question: the USSR and Vietnam once again were at the bottom of the list, a judgment not without merit.

As we just discussed on the topic of political stability and as table 4–5 suggests, it was those Americans most interested in international affairs who took the more extreme or committed view on the human-rights situation in most of these countries. For the USSR and Vietnam, this group was especially inclined to call the situation "very

unfavorable"—67 and 82 percent, respectively. In the case of the
Philippines, the surprisingly positive balance among the population
as a whole, commented on previously, was almost completely
reversed among those more interested in the world beyond our borders.

A few differences registered by other specific population groups
are worth noting.

Australia. The college educated, the more affluent, and members of
the professional and business community gave Australia well above
average "very favorable" ratings (eighteen to twenty-four year olds
were a bit more tempered here than the average). Black Americans
rated Australia substantially below the norm, another indication of
their skepticism about Australian racial and immigration policies.

China. The college educated were more negative than average.

Japan. The more affluent gave higher marks than average here, and
blacks less so.

Philippines. The more affluent were moderately more critical than
the norm.

South Korea. The college educated and the more affluent joined
those most interested in world affairs in viewing the situation more
negatively.

USSR. Blacks were much less *unfavorable* than average, although
still in the negative column by a strong majority (23–67 percent).

Taiwan. The more affluent were a bit more negative than the
national norm. More Americans said they have no opinion about the
human-rights situation in Taiwan than for any of the countries
tested.

Vietnam. Starting out with very poor overall ratings, Vietnam was
held in particularly poor esteem concerning human rights by the
twenty-five- to thirty-four-year-old age group (the one most directly
affected by the Vietnam war), the college educated, members of the
professional and business community, the clerical and sales force,

and, as we have already seen in table 4–5, those who follow foreign news most closely.

Human Rights: Voices of Experience

The focus on human rights was unquestionably one of the most controversial components of foreign policy of the Carter years. Both by speech and action, President Carter and many of his key appointees supported the cause of human rights with a fervor that at times took on the mantle of a sacred crusade. Through creation of a special bureau in the Department of State, and naming to head it an individual who took her mission seriously and pressed it with vigor, the Carter administration gave human rights a very special place in the foreign-policy network. An annual report, issued by the State Department, that rated human rights in countries around the world turned into a kind of international report card on what was going on globally in promoting the cause of this central feature of U.S. diplomacy.

The advent of Ronald Reagan to the presidency changed this, of course, and Mr. Reagan's first nominee to fill the State Department slot eventually withdrew his candidacy under heavy fire that included allegations that his commitment to the human-rights program was less than adequate. In addition, some of Mr. Reagan's first foreign visitors were from countries such as South Korea and Argentina, countries that had been special targets of his predecessor's criticisms.

Interviews and discussions with a number of persons who have spent many years in the foreign-affairs environment, whether officially or unofficially, in government or out, and from a varied intellectual and ideological background, have turned up a considerable degree of consensus on this subject—a consensus with which the author feels quite comfortable.

As a foreign-policy *goal,* the pursuit of human rights is admirable, appropriate, and very much in keeping with the sense of idealism and generosity that has given the United States much of its luster for peoples all over the globe. Of course, we should stand up for individual human rights, just as our forbears stood up for their own and those of their countrymen, leading to the founding of the republic in the first place. It is an ideal that speaks to the American soul.

Problems arise when that goal is turned into a *tool.* It is, as the Carter administration appeared to find out, a tool simpler to use against a government or ruling group in a country of lesser rather than greater power or significance. Certainly few would argue that the cause of human rights was applied toward Taiwan in a fashion not deemed appropriate to use with China. An opening foray against the USSR met with such a stern rebuff that the subject was not pursued with anything like the same vigor in the following months and years. But countries where our leverage was greater—on the Asian scene none is more obvious than South Korea because of the critical U.S. role in that nation's security—continued to feel the pressure of Washington in clear and at times, to them, insulting terms.

Human rights, it needs to be stressed, can and do encompass a broad range of issues: individual security, political freedom, and economic well-being, to mention but a few. And it is vital here to recognize differences in various social structures. For Americans, individual rights tend to be at the top of the list; our commitment to the collective entity is not nearly as strong as peoples living, for example, within a Confucian framework, a framework that holds major sway in parts of Asia. Furthermore, for many people pulling themselves out of poverty and just beginning to enjoy some of the fruits of local economic progress, such economic well-being is a human right of overriding proportions.

This is not to say that the United States should not remain strong in its support for the advancement of human rights in any and all appropriate forums, never ceasing to use available private and diplomatic channels. The United Nations and the ongoing, if stalemated deliberations of the 35-nation Conference on Security and Cooperation in Europe (the so-called "Helsinki Process") are examples that readily come to mind. But selective application (which often means, as suggested above, going after the relatively weaker and leaving alone the relatively stronger) can lead to confused signals among friend and foe alike, and can provoke a nationalistic backlash that hardly serves either U.S. interests or those of the country and its citizens where this response to our intervention is triggered.

Different societies are at different levels of economic, political, and social maturity. Our is not perfect. While continuing to champion the cause of human rights globally with tact and discretion, we also need to do more in terms of setting an example within our own borders—an example that makes our rhetoric more acceptable and less a manifestation of that arrogance of power about which our critics at home and abroad are wont to remind us.

5 Trade and Economic Relations with Asia

In 1977 the volume of U.S. trade with Asia for the first time surpassed the volume with Europe. Although the balance moved back in the other direction in 1978, it is inevitable that our burgeoning economic ties with various Asian nations will lead to a long-term dominance of trade levels by our trading partners across the Pacific.

The tendency, of course, is to think in terms of U.S. economic links with Japan, and it is true that our trade with Japan very clearly outstrips that with any other Asian nation—or any nation anywhere, for that matter, with the sole exception of Canada. Nonetheless, as table 5-1 shows, several other countries in Asia also trade with the United States in substantial volume. Indeed, of the 15 principal trading partners of United States around the world, four are found in Asia—Japan, Taiwan, South Korea, and Australia. In addition, the overall improvement of relations between the United States and China following normalization of formal diplomatic ties in January of 1979 has led to sharply increased trade with the People's Republic as well, although it trails far behind the leaders.

In assessing the importance of U.S. trade and economic relations with various Asian nations, it is not enough to focus just on the volume totals, impressive as they are in several instances. It is also instructive to note the degree to which the United States is a major factor in the overall economic life of almost every country in the region. For many of them, trade with the United States takes up one-fifth or more of their total foreign trade. This, in turn, means that economic conditions in the United States, and investment, purchasing, selling, or other related decisions taken here, assume unusually large meaning for our partners across the Pacific. It is small wonder then that many Asians can come to resent what they consider at times to be cavalier or condescending attitudes on the part of Americans doing business in Asia—either as government officials or as private participants. Such behavior overlooks, in the eyes of Asian observers, both the absolute figures involved and the relative impor-

Table 5-1
Trade: The United States and Asia

Country	Exports[a]	Imports[a]	Trade with U.S. as Percentage of Total	U.S. Balance[a]
Japan	20,574	30,701	22	− 10,127
Taiwan	4,301	6,849	31	− 2,548
South Korea	4,663	4,147	25	+ 516
Australia	4,059	2,509	17	+ 1,550
Indonesia	1,544	5,182	18	− 3,638
Singapore	3,004	1,920	14	+ 1,084
Philippines	1,987	1,730	26	+ 257
Malaysia	1,330	2,577	16	− 1,247
Thailand	1,255	815	14	+ 440
New Zealand	591	701	14	− 110
Vietnam	1	0.3	0.1	+ 0.7
China	3,749	1,053	10	+ 2,696
USSR	1,509	453	12	+ 1,056
Canada	34,102	41,455	67	− 7,353
Asia	50,400	78,848	—	− 28,448
World Total	216,592	240,830	—	− 24,238

Sources: *U.S. Exports, World Area by Commodity Grouping* (Washington, D.C.: U.S. Bureau of the Census, 1980); *U.S. General Imports, World Area by Commodity* (Washington, D.C.: U.S. Bureau of the Census, 1980); *Asia 1981 Yearbook, Far Eastern Economic Review,* courtesy of CoConveners of Williamsburg X.
[a]1980, million U.S. dollars.

tance these figures acquire in each of these countries. This condition plays an increasingly critical role in the expectation and insistence many Asian nations and peoples have that they be accorded a larger measure of respect and equality in their dealings with the United States.

Trade with Asia versus Europe

In the opening pages of this book, we considered the Eurocentric bias that tends to color the thinking of most Americans when they turn their eyes beyond our national borders. This inclination shows itself once again when respondents in our survey were asked a question about comparative trade levels between the United States and Europe, on one hand, and the United States and Asia, on the other. In fact, when given three alternatives from which to choose, respondents with an opinion were least inclined to choose the answer most nearly correct, that is, trade levels are about equal.

In terms of total U.S. foreign trade, including both exports and imports, which of the following statements do you think is most accurate?

U.S. trade with Europe is considerably larger than U.S. trade with Asia	35 percent
U.S. trade with Asia is considerably larger than U.S. trade with Europe.	29 percent
U.S. trade with Europe and Asia are about equal.	21 percent
Do not know.	15 percent

The largest percentage believed that our trade with Europe dominates. This is not surprising, given the fact that several indicators have already pointed to a general inclination in favor of European countries and the importance of Europe (other indicators still to be examined support this trend). Indeed, one might well have assumed that the proportion naming Europe as the larger trading partner would have been considerably higher.

Among some Americans presumably closer to the wellsprings of power, this was in fact the case. The college educated, the more affluent, and those who showed themselves to be very interested in international affairs all named Europe as the dominant partner in numbers well above the national norm. These same groups, however, also opted for Asia as the larger regional partner in proportions above the norm.

One can speculate that at least two determining factors are at work here. For those whose interests or knowledge is greater in one area or the other, that fact in itself—the very attraction of the area and enhanced awareness of it—may lead them to choose it as the more important. For others, higher-than-average levels of interest or knowledge may impel them to make a clear choice—one way or the other—and avoid the compromise alternative, the less categorical middle.

Familiarity with the area most definitely did lead the group of specialists and experts we interviewed to pick Asia as the dominant regional trading partner, and by a very large comparative margin. Thus, 66 percent (thirty-one of the forty-seven persons questioned) said U.S. trade with Asia was considerably larger than our trade with Europe, while only 4 percent picked Europe as the principal partner. (These percentages must be viewed as indicative only since the sample was so small that it cannot provide statistical reliability. Even so, the lopsidedness is striking.) For most of these individuals the tremendous potential that Asia holds in terms of natural resources, human skills, and expanding markets makes it the most exciting target for the future. It is a potential, however, that must be developed and cultivated with the utmost care, respect, and patience—a theme to which we will return.

Relative Product Quality

We have already seen that Americans tend to rank most Asian nations below a number of test countries elsewhere in the world in terms of favorable/unfavorable feelings, standard of living, and stability of the political situation. Does this general outlook hold for opinions on product quality as well? To find out, we asked the following:

> Using this scale, I would like you to tell me your attitude about the quality of products manufactured in different countries. If +5 represents a country that makes products of the very highest quality, and −5 a country whose products are of the lowest quality, how far up or down the scale would you rate the products of [country]?

The results are shown in table 5–2, listed in descending order according to those who ranked a country's product quality as "very high," that is, those who said either +5 or +4.

Following the usual pattern, Japan and Australia again led the list as far as nations in Asia are concerned, topped only by Canada (in first place for just about everything) and West Germany (ahead of Australia, but not Japan). For almost all other countries in Asia, ratings of the perceived quality of manufactured goods fell somewhere below those for liking or disliking a given country (table 1–1), on one hand, and above those for standard of living (table 4–1) on the other. Quality of products, unlike quality of life, was frequently rated above the level of political stability in Asian countries (table 4–3).

Table 5–2
Quality of Products

	Very High (Percentage)	Moderately High (Percentage)	Moderately Low (Percentage)	Very Low (Percentage)	Do Not Know (Percentage)
1. Canada	54	40	1	1	4
2. Japan	49	37	6	5	3
3. West Germany	48	39	6	2	5
4. Australia	29	55	4	1	11
5. Israel	21	53	13	3	10
6. Brazil	18	59	12	2	9
7. New Zealand	17	58	9	3	13
8. Saudi Arabia	15	46	19	9	11
9. China	14	56	18	5	7
10. Taiwan	12	53	22	8	5
11. Philippines	11	63	14	3	9
12. India	8	46	28	8	10
12. USSR	8	37	26	19	10
14. Singapore	6	51	23	6	14
14. South Korea	6	47	29	8	10
14. Thailand	6	46	27	9	12
17. Indonesia	5	42	30	6	17
18. Malaysia	4	41	30	5	20
18. Nigeria	4	40	32	7	17
20. Vietnam	3	25	37	22	13
21. North Korea	2	29	41	15	13

This listing reveals a good deal about certain American stereotypes, as well as reflecting some enormous shifts in public opinion over the years.

For those whose memories go back that far, Japan in the late 1930s was the country that, proverbially, "made toys that broke." Now it ranks on the list as a producer of high-quality products virtually tied with another former American military adversary, West Germany. And the relatively positive perception of China once again shows the effects of our newly opened romance with that former adversary, at a time when there are not yet too many goods available by which to judge their putative quality. (There is something of a parallel here, it can be argued, with the standing just above China of Saudi Arabia—a country that has, to all intents and purposes, just one product to sell, albeit of crucially important quality).

Several countries in Asia are given undeservably short shrift—primarily a reflection of ignorance as to their role as U.S. trading partner and supplier of many widely used commodities. In this group fall, at a minimum, Taiwan, Singapore, and South Korea, all of which have moved heavily into the American market but which have not yet gained recognition in any measure that approaches current reality. A Potomac Associates study on U.S.-Korean relations conducted in 1979, for example, found that only 16 percent of the American people were aware of the fact that Korea is one of our fifteen largest trading partners. We noted earlier that more than eight Americans in ten believe that the United States still supplies major economic aid to Korea, even though our aid program was phased out some years ago. Given such misinformation, it is no surprise that Korea, along with some other nations equally undeserving, is accorded low marks for product quality.

The traditional place ceded to Vietnam, the USSR, and North Korea again held firm; the core of Americans who looks upon those three countries in the most negative light gave them substantially the largest proportions of "very low" ratings.

On the subject of product quality, it can be added, Americans proved to be strikingly uniform in their views; meaningful differences among different population groups on this topic were few and far between.

The Import Threat and Protectionism

The extraordinary surge of Japanese automobile sales in the United States in the past few years, combined with growing competition either from Japan or many other countries in fields where the United States once was robust and self-confident—steel, textiles, and, especially, the multifaceted electronics industry, to name a few—have sparked heated debate. American industry, once the model of efficiency and productivity, has lagged seriously in some sectors, as rates of saving and capital investment have slowed and worker productivity has slumped.

The result has been a growing demand in some quarters for the imposition of protectionist measures to help flagging U.S. companies reestablish their international competitiveness. As of late 1981 such demands had not yet resulted in enactment of specific legislation by the U.S. Congress, but protectionist sentiment remained strong. Forces of free trade and protectionism were locked in serious debate, both within the Reagan administration and throughout the private sector, with the outcome in doubt. Indeed, several Asian nations had already entered into "voluntary quotas," as in the case of the Japanese automobile industry, or "orderly marketing agreements," for shipments of some textile products, footwear, and electronic equipment from Japan, South Korea, and Taiwan, for example. Adopted under intense U.S. pressure, and not at all to the liking of the industries affected in Asia, these devices were accepted only as an alternative to the possibility of harsher protectionist legislation emanating from Capitol Hill.

Americans, we have found, are very conscious of the threat of foreign imports, with Japan in particular being the prime target of their concern. This became apparent when we asked respondents in our national survey to turn their attention to several countries around the world as actual or potential sources of harm to American workers:

> The United States imports large quantities of goods from many countries around the world for sale here. In the case of countries listed on this card, do you think imports from any of them pose a serious threat *now* to the jobs of American workers? Please tell me which countries, if any, pose such a serious threat *today*.

> And what about *five or ten years* from now? Please tell me which countries, if any, will pose a serious threat to the jobs of American workers *then*.

Japan, the principal culprit, led its closest current competitor by margins at or close to two to one for both the present and the future (table 5-3). Taiwan, clearly in second place as a perceived threat to American workers today, was joined by West Germany and China as the second most worrisome foreign competitors by the end of the decade.

China, straining under grandiose development plans that have had to be cut back in the face of vexatious and not immediately resolvable economic realities, is the only country among those listed seen as a much larger potential than actual threat. This finding reflects an awareness on the part of Americans that might come as a surprise to those who tend to dismiss the public as being so generally uninformed on world affairs as not to have views worth taking into account. Thus the Chinese threat, which is in fact more potential than actual, is seen as a serious concern in the future by almost twice as many respondents as see it that way now.

On this issue, those who are very interested in international

Table 5–3
Countries Whose Imports Pose Serious Threat to U.S. Jobs
(percentage)

	Today *(Percentage)*	*Five or Ten Years from now* *(Percentage)*
1. Japan	76	62
2. Taiwan	44	31
3. West Germany	29	30
4. China	18	33
5. Mexico	18	23
6. South Korea	16	14
7. Brazil	6	9
8. Canada	5	6
9. Australia	5	6
10. Nigeria	2	3
None	8	9

affairs drew a clear—and, I would surmise, probably accurate—distinction between the current and potential threats presented by China and Taiwan. Eight percent of these individuals saw China as a serious threat at present, while 53 percent viewed Taiwan in this light—a ratio of almost seven to one against Taiwan. Looking ahead five or ten years, however, 33 percent of this group perceived competition from China as a serious problem for American workers (a fourfold increase), whereas the number who saw Taiwan that way had dropped almost in half, to 29 percent—marginally below the figure for China.

South Korea, generally plagued by a bad reputation among many Americans, for once was spared such opprobrium on this topic: relatively small proportions looked upon it as harmful to the interest of workers here. In part, of course, this is simply due to the very low American awareness of Korea's economic development, which has moved it into a position of considerable importance to the United States as a trading partner. As Korean goods become more visible to American consumers, and as Korea sheds its reputation as an under-developed "client" state, one of the side-effects likely will be an increased degree of public concern about its potentially damaging role vis-a-vis our domestic work force.

For a change, Canada and Australia failed to assume their customary high-ranking positions. In a sense, to be sure, they did since the fewer the mentions here, the more positive (or less worried) the respondent's attitude. Australia, it might be pointed out, is the largest exporter of beef to the United States and as such contributes to the American job market through its involvement in, among other things, the fast-food business. Australia also has the largest net deficit among the nations of Asia in its trade with the United States, which puts it at the opposite end of the spectrum from Japan.

The case of Japan as a perceived threat to the interests of American workers represent an apparent contradiction or anomaly in overall attitudes. How, after all, can Japan be seen by three Americans in four as constituting a present *serious* threat to jobs here and yet be ranked near the top of many of the evaluative indicators we have examined thus far? Does not the job-threat issue influence other feelings? Do Americans not see a link between this issue and others and draw some logical conclusions? The answer, at least as of the time of this writing, I believe is twofold.

The quick response is "not yet." Whether that can remain the case indefinitely, if the import and balance-of-payments issues continue to cloud the air and come to be seen as causing clear and irrefutable economic hardship in certain sectors of this country, is doubtful. The potential then for falloff in the high ratings given Japan—especially in the area of like/dislike and in support for Japan's security, to be discussed in the next chapter—is very real. It is safe to say that much of the concerned leadership in both the United States and Japan—both public and private—is well aware of the dangers involved here. Although there is no agreement or consensus on what needs to be done, the level of attention these problems are receiving is at least a step in the right direction.

There is another side. The fact is that many Americans have a high measure of respect for Japan and the Japanese. (Remember that in terms of personal stereotypes, Japanese tended to conform in Americans' eyes, along with Australians, most closely to a hypothetical ideal.) Americans also certainly value Japanese products highly—Japan is second only to Canada among those who say that the quality of its products is "very high."

This is both a spectacular turnabout and a major accomplishment. What the Japanese have gained from many, and perhaps most, Americans is a kind of grudging respect. Japanese have become, it might be said only in part facetiously, the "Asian Yankees."

The turnabout in American opinion that has brought to Japan and the Japanese such admiration and respect is not immutable, just as no opinion is. Should the problem areas just mentioned persist and cause these positive attitudes to deteriorate, then the well-used rallying cry of "Yankee go home" could be turned around and used by Americans themselves against the Asian Yankees.

Economic Ties: Voices of Experience

We noted earlier in this chapter that a selected group of individuals with long and direct experience in Asia held the prevalent view that our trade with Asian nations exceeded that with countries of Europe by a considerable margin. Although that is an exaggeration of the present state of affairs, their assessment will almost certainly be borne out in coming years.

With almost no exeptions, these people look to Asia as an area of enormous potential as far as American economic interests are concerned—if we handle our dealings carefully and fairly, and exert pressure where appropriate for similar treatment from our Asian partners. In particular, the feeling was expressed by just about everyone interviewed that protectionism in the face of strong Asian competition is not the answer. "Protectionism is a form of saving a cripple," one observer noted, with another adding, "In the end, it is the American consumer who pays." (One individual with considerable experience on Capitol Hill took sharp exception to the general shape of opinion here. As he put it, "Fair trade requires protectionism. Free our industries from overburdensome government regulations, and put up trade barriers to get our house cleaned up.")

This virtually unanimous strong opposition to protectionism was not voiced in a total vacuum, however, unrelated to current political and economic conditions. Given the plight of some American industries, domestic political realities may (and indeed have) made some restrictions inevitable. The sales quotas and orderly marketing agreements referred to above are, after all, restrictions by another name. Ultimately, the goal should be provision of the freest access possible to markets both here and on the other side of the Pacific—a goal that will require patience and considerable negotiating skills.

Part of the problem for some American industries today as they try to deal in Asia is right here at home. To be sure, a variety of restrictive practices adopted by some countries in Asia has made it much more difficult than would otherwise be the case for American firms trying to do business there. Subtle licensing requirements, long delays in customs inspection, requirements for arcane documentation—these and other so-called nontariff barriers have given many American businessmen fits and have led them to call on the U.S. government to insist on fair access from those countries that have resorted to such tactics. Japan, of course, has been singled out for particular blame in this regard, although the situation there has improved for some, but not all sectors.

What has been a major problem for American firms is a lack of aggressiveness in trying to penetrate Asian markets. Among other things, this requires that much more attention be given to understanding how individual Asian markets work—learning, for example, the ways of the Japanese trading companies and how to mesh American exports efforts with their ways and techniques of doing business. The American economy as a whole, and many of its component parts to the highest degree, have not been all that export oriented. Many nations in Asia (and elsewhere, of course) must trade to live. For us foreign trade has been a vital necessity, to be sure, but still a relatively small piece of our overall economic activity.

A number of steps, which will be spelled out in greater detail in later pages, are called for. But let it be said that a larger intellectual investment in the Asian marketplace, longer tours of duty for businessmen assigned to the region, language and area study, and a careful examination of laws on our statute books that hinder trade and exports are all needed. So is a strengthening of our federal commercial service, the overseas arm of the Department of Commerce and its activities in assisting American businessmen and others working abroad.

Additionally, as one observer after another noted, the American economy and American enterprise must be put back into shape. Years of inadequate investment in plant renewal, research and development, and lack of introduction of new, more efficient techniques have served to put many American industries in a disastrously weakened competitive position compared with some of their Asian counterparts. I have heard the complaint voiced frequently in Asia, and in Japan with predictable regularity, that industries and enterprises there have accomplished in recent decades—and certainly since the end of World War II—precisely what we had been urging; modernization, rapid growth, and a general rebuilding of their economies on a scale that has made them genuine regional or global economic powers. In the meantime, they say, we have lagged behind, complacent, overconfident, and suffering from a loss of the drive, ambition, and ingenuity that were once the envy of the globe. Now, when the results of these parallel developments are coming to haunt us, we all too often cry "unfair!" and call for retaliations and restrictions. It is time, they say, for us to get about the urgent task of putting our own house in order—a sentiment very much shared by most of our expert commentators here.

As indicated earlier, there are a number of specific steps that might be taken both here and in Asian countries to improve market access and promote expanded trade within the region. Along with other policy and programmatic recommendations called for by some of the findings in earlier chapters, these will be treated in detail in the closing sections of this book. Before we get to that, however, let us first turn to yet another area of contention and concern—political ties and security commitments.

6 Political Ties and Security Commitments

The last three major wars in which the United States was a full participant and in which many Americans gave their lives started for us in Asia. Even today some of the most dangerous global flashpoints are in Asia—the Sino-Soviet border, the Korean peninsula, the border between Vietnam and China, and the border between Vietnam-occupied Cambodia and Thailand. The Straits of Formosa, while relatively calm, cannot be overlooked as another potential locus of military action, with Beijing maintaining its claim to Taiwan as part of the People's Republic and Taipei maintaining its claim as the rightful inheritor of Chinese sovereignty.

Beyond these security considerations are the vital economic stakes touched on in the last chapter. The Straits of Malacca, far less well known to Americans, one can presume, than the Straits of Hormuz, are one of the vital waterways of the world and the ocean lifeline for many of the countries we are discussing in these pages. With the balance of our trade shifting toward Asia, the importance of these various security, economic, and related political ties, threats, or rivalries cannot be underestimated. Our own future as a global power is inextricably and increasingly tied in with the future of Asia.

In the wake of defeat in Vietnam and the widespread antiwar movement in the United States, there has been much discussion and heated debate in recent years as to whether Americans have lost their will to fight and are no longer ready to defend friends and stand up to foes. The assumption in many quarters seems to be that we as a people have growth tired of security commitments, are increasingly inward-looking, and would be happier retreating into some kind of "Fortress America."

Two series of public-opinion surveys conducted over a number of years provide some highly illuminating trends suggesting that this is not, or certainly is no longer, the case. Speculation about the demise of American political will appears premature. Thus growth in isolationist sentiment and a comparable decline in internationalist views, which had been observable since the mid-1960s, came to a halt in the middle of the seventies and showed clear signs of reversal at the beginning of our current decade.

Furthermore, particularly since the midseventies, Americans have expressed themselves in increasing numbers as prepared to come to the defense of many of their friends should they come under armed attack.

Americans: Isolationist or Internationalist?

To get a reading on relative levels of internationalist as opposed to isolationist or neoisolationist points of view, we have periodically asked cross-sections of the public whether they agree or disagree with a series of statements concerning the basic international orientation of the United States.[1] In the questionnaire the various statements were intermingled to reduce bias; to facilitate our analysis, however, we first list those statements involving an isolationist or unilateral approach and then those characterized by an internationalist or multilateral point of view:

A. Since the United States is the most powerful nation in the world, we should go our own way in international matters, not worrying too much about whether other countries agree with us or not.

	1964	1968	1972	1974	1976	1980
Agree	19%	23%	22%	32%	29%	26%
Disagree	70	72	72	57	62	66
Do not know	11	5	6	11	9	8

In 1980, two Americans in three disagreed, a proportion above that registered in 1974 and 1976 but still below the peak reached in the period from 1964 through 1972. The year that this statement was most favored by Americans was 1974.

B. The United States should mind its own business internationally and let other countries get along as best they can on their own.

	1964	1968	1972	1974	1976	1980
Agree	18%	27%	35%	41%	41%	30%
Disagree	70	66	56	47	49	61
Do not know	12	7	9	12	10	9

Americans rejected this concept, even more unilateralist in character, more decisively in 1980 than at any time since 1968.

C. We should not think so much in international terms but concentrate more on our own national problems and building up our strength and prosperity here at home.

	1964	1968	1972	1974	1976	1980
Agree	55	60	73	77	73	61
Disagree	32	31	20	14	22	30
Do not know	13	9	7	9	5	9

The proportion that agreed with the unilateralist stance on this proposition in 1980 was lower than in any year since 1968. This notion was most in favor in 1974, the same as for statement A and statement B (tied, in the latter case, with 1976).

D. The United States should cooperate fully with the United Nations.

	1964	1968	1972	1974	1976	1980
Agree	72	72	63	66	46	59
Disagree	16	21	28	20	41	28
Do not know	12	7	9	14	13	13

Support for the United Nations hit its low point, quite clearly, in 1976. A Gallup Poll released in December of 1975 pinpointed the cause: "The public's rating of the United Nations' performance has declined to a thirty-year low following passage of a resolution condemning Zionism as a 'form of racism and racial discrimination' ". The substantial comeback recorded in 1980 probably stemmed in part from very broad backing in the United Nations for resolutions condemning the seizure of American hostages in Iran and the Soviet invasion of Afghanistan. Even so, it should be noted, support for the United Nations remained lower than it had been for the decade spanning the midsixties to the midseventies.

E. In deciding its foreign policies, the United States should take into account the views of its major allies.

	1964	1968	1972	1974	1976	1980
Agree	81%	84%	80%	69%	72%	79%
Disagree	7	9	12	16	18	13
Do not know	12	7	8	15	10	8

Agreement with the proposition that we should consult closely with our allies climbed ten points between 1974 and 1980, returning it to levels near those that held between 1964 and 1972.

We also found dramatic increase in support for defense of allies in West Europe and Japan, the two final propositions included in this series (beginning in 1972).

F. The United States should come to the defense of its major European allies with military force if any of them are attacked by the USSR.

	1972	1974	1976	1980
Agree	52	48	56	70
Disagree	32	34	27	17
Do not know	16	18	17	13

G. The United States should come to the defense of Japan with military force if it is attacked by the USSR or the People's Republic of China.

	1972	1974	1976	1980
Agree	43	37	45	57
Disagree	40	42	37	24
Do not know	17	21	18	19

Once again 1974 was the year of least support for coming militarily to the defense of Japan or our European allies; clear majorities were in favor of such action in 1980, with more Americans agreeing with the proposition in each case than at any previous point in our testings of opinion.

Utilizing a system first devised by my colleague Lloyd A. Free for the Institute of International Social Research in 1964, we can take reactions to the statements listed above to place Americans on an internationalist-isolationist spectrum. To qualify as "completely internationalist" a respondent had to disagree with the notions that the United States should go its own way (A), mind its own business (B), and concentrate more on national problems (C), while agreeing that the United States should cooperate with the United Nations (D), take into account the views of its allies (E), and come to the defense of Western Europe (F) and Japan (G). To be classified as "completely isolationist," a respondent had to give precisely the opposite

answers. Categories were also provided for "predominantly internationalist" and "predominantly isolationist" (meaning conformity to
the "completely" patterns in most but all respects) and "mixed"
(meaning a relatively even mixture of internationalist and isolationist
patterns).

The comparative results of this compilation, shown over a period
of sixteen years, are set forth in figure 6-1.

Trends over the years are both striking and impressive and should
provide some reassurance to those who worry about American will.
There was, to be sure, an uninterrupted drop in the number of those
whom we classified as "total internationalists" over the years 1964,
1968, 1972, and 1974 (65, 59, 56, and 41 percent, respectively). But
the trend reversed itself in 1976, with 44 percent moving into this
category; by 1980 it had reached a clear majority of 61 percent.

For "total isolationists," although the number in 1980 was marginally larger than during the years 1964-1972, it had dropped well
below the levels of 1974 and 1976.

A retreat into "Fortress America" is not what most Americans
want. Especially in the aftermath of Vietnam, Americans came to a
fundamentally sober assessment of the world scene. Recognizing the
failure in Vietnam, they came to the judgment that we must be more
careful about the range of our commitments; those that are worth-
while and held to be strongly in the national interest must be
defended with U.S. might.

Security Commitments: How Strong?

As we have just seen, the relative growth in the sense of internationalism over the past half-decade stemmed in part from renewed willingness of Americans to defend certain key friends and allies. Along
with the series of surveys measuring internationalist-isolationist
trends, we have probed separately and specifically into the issue of
security commitments.[2] This series has in recent years gone beyond
defense of Japan and Europe to include other countries as well:

Please tell me whether you agree or disagree with the following statements:
The United States should come to the defense of country A with military
force if it is attacked by country B.

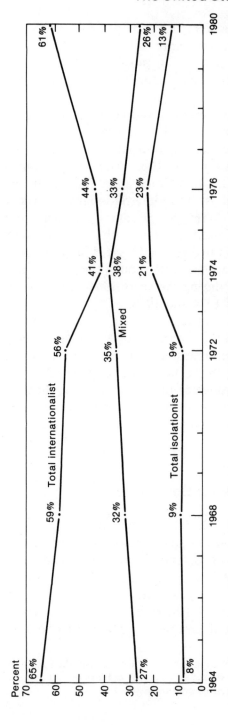

Figure 6-1. Internationalist/Isolationist Trends, 1964–1980

Source: Potomac Associates data, 1964, 1968, 1972, 1974, 1976, and 1980; Lloyd A. Free and William Watts, "Internationalism Comes of Age—Again," *Public Opinion*, April/May 1980, p. 49. Reprinted with permission.

The country (or countries) listed first in table 6-1 is the one Americans were asked to defend. The country (or countries) in parentheses is the aggressor.[3]

Looking first at the defense of "major European allies" and Japan, for which there are data going back to 1972, it appears that a turning point was reached around 1974. From a low in that year of 48 percent of Americans agreeing that we should come to the defense of friends in Europe if attacked by the USSR, and an actual plurality of 42-37 percent opposed to coming to the defense of Japan, support has climbed steadily to current very substantial majorities—almost three-quarters of the population favored defense of Europe and almost seven in ten felt the same way about Japan. These are impressive numbers endorsing the use of our military force to back certain key allies.

In the case of Europe, support was especially high among the college educated and those "very interested" in international affairs (reaching 89 percent among the latter). For Japan, both of these groups (with the "very interested" at the same level of 89 percent) and members of the professional and business community and the more affluent expressed substantially higher-than-average support. Those with only a grade-school education and blacks were considerably less in agreement than the national norm, a position they took consistently for all the security questions.

For other countries, obviously, the picture varies. Australia and the Philippines both commanded clear majority support for their defense. The use of the term "enemy of the United States" as the potential attacker may have served to shift the balance slightly more in the favor of these nations; it will be recalled, however, that Australia and, to a lesser degree, the Philippines have registered well on other indicators in our study, which would be consistent with these levels of support for their defense. The college educated, more affluent, and "very interested" were particularly high in their backing for Australia, with the last group also above average as far as the Philippines was concerned.

Support for defense of Taiwan in the event of attack by the People's Republic increased noticeably between 1978 and 1980, bringing it to a bare plurality. As another example of the remarkable turnabout in attitudes concerning China, there is actually a slightly larger plurality (but one that is not statistically significant) in favor of providing such military support to the People's Republic if it is attacked by the USSR!

Table 6-1
Defense of Certain Countries if Attacked

	1972 (Percentage)	1974 (Percentage)	1975 (Percentage)	1976 (Percentage)	1978 (Percentage)	1979 (Percentage)	1980 (Percentage)
Major European allies (if attacked by USSR)	52ᵃ	48	48	56	62	64	74
	32ᵇ	34	34	27	26	26	19
	16ᶜ	18	18	17	12	10	7
Australia (enemy of United States)							70
							21
							9
Japan (USSR or China)	43	37	42	45	50	54	68
	40	42	39	37	35	35	28
	17	21	19	18	15	11	4
Philippines (enemy of United States)							65
							25
							10
China (USSR)							45
							42
							13
Taiwan (China)					32	34	43
					48	51	42
					20	15	15
South Korea (North Korea)					32	32	38
					52	56	51
					16	12	11
Thailand (Vietnam)							30
							55
							15

ᵃTop number indicates percentage agreeing.
ᵇMiddle number indicates percentage disagreeing.
ᶜBottom number indicates percentage who do not know.

The two countries that fared worst in terms of defense support by Americans are South Korea and Thailand. Both countries, as we have seen in earlier pages, rank well down the list in the perceptions of Americans concerning like/dislike, quality of life, quality of products, political stability, and stated levels of knowledge. Many Americans hold negative stereotypes concerning the Korean people. Both are continental Asian countries. After Vietnam, many Americans may be less willing to enter into another land war in that part of the world on behalf of countries not held in particularly high esteem than to come to the defense of other Asian nations not a part of the land mass—and about whom overall perceptions are considerably more favorable to begin with.

Consideration of American commitments and interests in Asia—under whatever rubric they may fall, whether it be political, economic, security, or something else—must be viewed in a variety of contexts, ranging from bilateral to multilateral, regional, and pan-Asian. Let us now turn to some of the most important of these, with the assessments in the pages that follow drawing heavily not only on the national survey but also on the views of our panel of experts and specialists.

Japan and Regional Security

Along with the problem of Japan's overwhelmingly favorable balance of trade with the United States, which manifests itself most visibly in Japanese domination of foreign automobile sales in the United States, the issue of Japan's appropriate security role has come to trouble bilateral relations in increasingly contentious fashion.

Japanese are puzzled and frequently irritated by our unremitting pressure. In their view it is unfair, even dangerous, to increase significantly the level of their defense spending since it could trigger a nationalist outburst of tragic consequences. At a conference in Tokyo in December of 1980, I was more than a little startled to have a highly respected Japanese public figure ask me rhetorically in the middle of a discussion of this topic, "Don't you Americans remember Pearl Harbor?"

Not only that, but we must keep in mind the fact that the very strong Japanese antiwar sentiment has been sanctioned by a Constitution imposed by American occupation authorities and has been seared into their national consciousness by our nuclear bombings.

On the other side of the coin, many Americans, including many in key policy positions, feel that the United States is already doing more than its fair share of carrying the defense burden of the free world. Japan, in particular, with a relatively small proportion of its gross national product (GNP) allocated to the defense sector, can and should do more. It is, after all, the American military shield that provides Japan the security that has fostered its spectacular economic growth. Why does it not do more? Why the "free ride," critics ask?

Our survey included a question on this topic, one that had been used once before and that was also posed to our leadership segment:

Under the provisions of the Japanese constitution approved by the American military occupation after World War II, Japan can have only limited military forces for defense. Some Americans believe that Japan should contribute more toward its own defense, and not continue to depend so heavily on the United States. Other Americans feel that a rearmed Japan might become a threat to the security of our allies. How do you, yourself, feel about this: do you think Japan should build up a larger military force for defense, or not?

	1978 All Adults	1980 All Adults	Leaders
Should build larger military force	46%	53%	76%
Should not	37	36	13
Do not know	17	11	11

Let us deal first with the total national results.

Shifts in opinion on Japanese rearmament during the period in question were relatively minor. What had been a plurality not much short of a majority in favor in 1978 became a slight majority two years later. Opposition levels remained essentially unchanged. The China euphoria that had led, as we shall see next, to a very real increase in support for some kind of military connection with Asia's most populous power had not been accompanied by a similar surge in support for more rearmament by Asia's economic superpower.

Those most supportive of higher levels of defense spending on Japan's part included the college educated, the more affluent, and, most of all, those very interested in international affairs, who favored this development by a margin of 68-26 percent. On the basis of age, younger Americans (eighteen to twenty-four year olds) were the most cautious—50-42 percent in favor—while the senior age

group in our study (fifty years of age and over) was more supportive—56–32 percent in agreement. World War II memories based on
age do not seem to be a strong factor here.

The fact that the number of those who expressed themselves
ready to come to the defense of Japan considerably exceeded the
number of those who approve of increased Japanese rearmament
may at first appear as a bit of an oddity.

At least part of the answer is to be found in the aversion most
Americans have for foreign aid, especially military assistance.
Because of the broad opposition to this kind of federal expenditure,
any testing of national sentiment on support for foreign military
assistance, or, as in the case of Japan, rearmament (which, it could
be assumed, might involve U.S. assistance) is likely to show a public
that is cautious and tempered at best in its enthusiasm. Part of this
reaction also may stem from the belief that, by encouraging arms
buildups—even among good friends—we are increasing the likeli-
hood of arms misuse, quite possibly at our own direct expense. And
here, to be sure, a possible "Pearl Harbor syndrome" could come
into play, with those Americans who are against increased Japanese
arms capabilities taking that view with history very much in mind.

In the case of coming to the defense of friends and allies, on the
other hand, the rationale for action is substantially altered. Americans are more willing to accept the logic, and resulting necessity, that
by protecting our own best friends we protect our own best interests.
This will result, as we have just seen, in considerable selectivity in
choosing among those we are asked to defend. A variety of factors,
many of which we have been examining in these pages, provide the
basis for the selections Americans tend to make.

Among the special leadership group, support for increased Japanese defense spending was markedly higher, although the percentage
must be treated with caution because of the small sample involved.

Undoubtedly the dominant feeling within this number of knowl-
edgeable individuals was the sense that Japan can in fact play a considerably larger regional role in terms of its own self-defense and the
security of its territorial waters. Thus support for increased defense
spending was generally linked to a very clear understanding that
Japan should not extend its activities much beyond defense of the
home islands and securing of the seas to some reasonable distance
from land. To go beyond and undertake any forward deployments
would almost certainly evoke memories of World War II, something

neither the Japanese nor their neighbors want. Such a buildup, which could include increased antisubmarine and minesweeping activities, for example, could be managed in a nonthreatening way and within the Japanese constitutional framework, two aspects of dealing with this highly emotional issue that must be taken carefully into account and not violated, lest there be a fearful and unwanted backlash.

The emotional subject of defense spending in Japan also presents a valuable lesson in the problem of intercultural relations. The Japanese concept of *ringi,* or decision making by consensus, is not a part of our thinking. Within Japanese society, both governors and governed must move slowly and very much in tandem when contemplating a shift of the magnitude represented by any significant amplification of Japan's security role. Many experienced observers would argue (and I agree with them) that this consensus-building process is now very much underway in Japan. Slowly but surely, the mood is becoming more accepting (if not enthusiastic) for Japan's playing a larger security role, although the limits and parameters of that role are not close to being determined. As this process unfolds itself, excessive outside pressure is likely to be counterproductive and lead to a stubborn and prideful negativism that will accomplish just the opposite of what is wanted by those who do believe that Japan's global stakes require some meaningful increase in its regional security contribution.

The free-ride concern, it has been pointed out, can overlook or at least minimize some important facts. Japan already has the eighth largest defense budget in the world, and its contributions tend to get little notice in the wake of the continuing criticism it receives for limiting its expenditures to something under 1 percent of GNP. The Japanese themselves also argue that they are beginning to do more both in Asia and elsewhere to support economic and social growth and thus free up local resources so that recipient countries can apply them to their own defense—something they might not have been able to do without Japanese economic assistance.

In the last analysis, however, it is clear that preponderant opinion among those dealing most directly with Japan and who have a sharper sense of the realities and requirements of the area is that Japan should reexamine its priorities with a realization borne of its expanding global role and power. Because of its remarkable economic success, it owes its immediate neighbors and friends and supporters, wherever they may be, a higher level of commitment to regional stability. One aspect of this can be enhanced support for U.S. efforts in the area (in Korea as well as in Japan), greater burden sharing, and perhaps a more specific degree of common-defense planning. If Japan comes to be perceived as unwilling to meet legitimate regional requirements and at the same time is viewed as continuing its spectacular economic development under the military protection of others, then discussions on this subject could easily assume a nasty and generally tendentious tone.

China, Arms, and New Directions

An announcement was made during the June 1980 visit to China of the American Secretary of State that the Reagan administration had made known its willingness to sell lethal military equipment to the People's Republic. This was the latest in a series of giant steps in U.S.-Chinese relations following the initial breakthrough during the Nixon presidency and the decision to establish full diplomatic ties by President Carter. It was a step fraught with controversy, and one that has moved the Washington-Beijing link into new untested, and potentially turbulent waters.

American opinion, it can be said, had moved in a generally supportive direction prior to the Reagan administration announcement, although expert opinion was predominantly on the other side of the fence. This judgment emerges from responses to a question on military support for China, asked both in our new study and in two previous samplings of attitudes:

Mainland China [The use of the term "Mainland China" stems from the fact that this wording had been used before and was required here to maintain statistical comparability.] is anxious to prevent the increase of Soviet power and influence in Asia and other parts of the world. Although we have fundamental differences with Mainland China, do you think the United States should help China build up its military strength to resist Soviet power and influence, or should we not help China in this way?

	1977 All Adults	1979 All Adults	1980 All Adults	Leaders
Assist China	11%	23%	47%	26%
Not help China	70	64	40	49

Do not know	19	13	13	2
(Heavily				
qualified and				
cautious)				23

The dazzling turnabout in attitudes toward China, documented elsewhere in this book, was demonstrated here once again, among the populace at large, at least. What had been overwhelming seven-to-one opposition to the idea of providing military assistance to China in 1977 had become a slight plurality in favor of such a proposition by the summer of 1980. The new results coincided almost exactly with levels of support for the defense of China if attacked by the USSR, shown in table 6-1.

Two groups showed more than average support for such assistance to China in our latest survey: younger Americans (eighteen to twenty-four year olds, who were partial to China in other areas as well), and those who proved to be somewhat interested in international affairs. Among those more opposed were members of the professional and business community and (by a bare majority) Americans aged thirty-five to forty-nine. It is possible that those in their late thirties and forties carry sharper memories of the Korean War and our combat with China at that time, leading them to be more cautious on this issue.

If caution was a factor in the thinking of this particular age group, it was the primary concern expressed by our "voices of experience." Even most of those who agreed with the idea said military assistance to China should be developed carefully, step by step, and, if possible, in such a way as to avoid unnecessary and gratuitous provocation of the USSR.

For many of those who saw a direct military link-up with China as not in our interests, this concern with the impact of such a step on the USSR was indeed paramount. Given Moscow's paranoia about Beijing, its motives, and its activities (a paranoia fully shared in the opposite direction, to be sure), then policy steps on our part that could be seen as closing some kind of regional noose around the USSR could make our dealings with the leaders in the Kremlin only more difficult than they already are.

Other notes of caution were sounded that are worth listening to, not only as they related to the opening of a direct military link between the United States and the People's Republic of China but as they touched on the overall shape of Sino-American relations and the possibility of a closer trilateral association that would include Japan.

Internal developments in China have been marked over the years by extreme unpredictability. That unpredictability has been every bit as much in evidence following the death of Mao Zedong as during his rule. Massive new plans associated with the "four modernizations" (priority of development for agriculture, industry, science and technology, and national defense) were curtailed, and many foreign companies who thought that China represented the greatest new economic bonanza in a long time found themselves frustrated and chastened by a general slowdown. Under the circumstances, it can be argued that U.S. policy toward China, both official and private, should be marked with caution, and recognition of uncertainty about the direction or directions on which China has embarked, and the durability they possess.

One practical consequence of moving too rapidly in the development of our relations with Beijing is that we stand to lose some measure of our flexibility. To the extent that we rush to meet all of China's desires, without being clear about our own, we tend to deal away our negotiating hand. And, as noted previously, we do this at the expense of foreclosing some of our options with the USSR.

It is important to keep in mind the genuine political and social differences that exist between the United States and the People's Republic—differences that a visitor to China is directly and frequently reminded of in any serious discussion with Chinese officials and colleagues. The cornerstone of U.S. policy in Asia remains Japan, and it is crucial that American and Japanese officials, who do not share the same troubling set of political and social differences, understand what the other is doing as they deal with Asia's geographic giant. The Japanese expect such ongoing consultation, even while they show little interest in developing a more integrated trilateral link. Indeed, any such partnership between China, Japan, and the United States would be viewed with considerable apprehension by all our friends in the region (and elsewhere as well, particularly in Europe), and with outright alarm by our adversaries.

It is impossible to leave any discussion of China and the future of our relations with it without mentioning the unsettled issue of Taiwan. What the ultimate solution of the status of Taiwan will be and how the linkage between the mainland and the island offshore will be worked out remain a mystery. Prophecies of doom for

Taiwan, following derecognition by the United States and our con-
summation of formal relations with the People's Republic, have been
proved remarkably wide of the mark. It is important to note that the
attitudes of Americans toward Taiwan and its people have been
maintained at a consistently high level, equal or close to those for
China and its people. Americans in general, and our group of
experts, policymakers, and specialists in particular, accepted the reality and importance of our burgeoning ties with the People's Republic. But they also looked to a continuation of U.S. support for the
legitimate rights and security of the people of Taiwan. Anything less
from us would be unworthy, even as we should acknowledge the cer-
tainty that eventually the Chinese, all the Chinese, in their own time
and in their unique Chinese way, will fashion their own resolution.
The series of proposals pointing toward unification, put forward by
the People's Republic in the fall of 1981, and promptly rejected by
Taiwan, was but the latest step in a complicated scenario whose outcome remains to be seen.

Korea: Asian Flashpoint

The potential threat represented by the continued division of the
Korean peninsula between two sharply hostile governments hardly
needs to be emphasized. It is one place on the globe where the specific interests of the United States, the USSR, China, and Japan are
all directly involved. Renewed warfare between North and South
Korea carries with it the prospect of wider and possibly catastrophic
conflict.

The American people, as virtually every indicator in this book
has suggested, do not hold South Korea and its people in very high
esteem. They relegate North Korea to the status of pariah, along with
other especially odious (to Americans) nations such as Vietnam and
the USSR. This overall lack of warmth for South Korea—which con-
siders itself one of the United States' best friends, important economic partner, strong supporter in international forums, and willing
ally when called upon for assistance during the Vietnam War—puz-
zles and worries the South Korean leadership, not least for the fact
that it has resulted in majority opposition among Americans to
defense of South Korea should the North decide to attack again.

Thoughtful Korean officials and others concerned with the
U.S.-Korean relationship are also acutely conscious of some of the

reasons for this coolness. "Koreagate," Reverend Moon and the Unification Church, and a virtual obsession on the part of foreign-media representatives (especially, Koreans say, Americans and Japanese) with reporting domestic political unrest but almost entirely overlooking major economic achievements—these and other factors hardly help.

Yet, as most of our experts agreed, Korean security and our own are linked, most obviously as stability on the peninsula affects the stability of Japan. Under the circumstances, there was essential unanimity on the need for the United States to maintain its forces in South Korea, approximately at the current level. This represents a clear signal not only to North Korea but to the USSR and China as well, of our commitment to peace in the area. This commitment may in fact be particularly important at this time and in the immediate future, when there is great uncertainty as to the motives of the aging leader of North Korea, Kim Il-sung. Any action, U.S. troop withdrawal especially, that gave Kim encouragement to think he could mount another invasion free of U.S. involvement should be carefully avoided.

South Korea has been a prime target for those who have advocated a highly visible U.S. human-rights policy. It is worth noting that many of the leadership figures we interviewed called for considerable restraint on this topic. While not denying that the issue is a legitimate one, they argued that the policy should not be applied dogmatically and that quiet but serious and respectful diplomacy may be more appropriate and effective. The same applies for the larger question of democratization and civilian control, developments that we should make clear we believe to be important but understanding and remembering our different cultures and strategic situations. Downtown Seoul, South Korea's capital, is about the same distance from the demilitarized line that divides South and North Korea as downtown Washington, D.C., is from Dulles International Airport. How would we feel if an implacable enemy, one that had made clear its intent to prevail over us in the end (the USSR, say) were located at that distance from the nation's capital? While such a situation does not provide a rationale for condoning any and all governmental actions on the part of the Republic of Korea, it certainly poses an important security consideration in the governing of the country and injects a psychological factor that cannot be overlooked or dismissed as trivial.

While little hope was held out for any near-term resolution of the

North-South impasse and for reunification of the peninsula, consistent support was expressed for regular encouragement from Washington for promoting the North-South dialogue. Such support could take the form of regular diplomatic contacts with the South Korean government and with authorities in Beijing and Moscow as well. Cross-recognition, along the lines of the German situation, should be a consistent goal, an objective that could reduce tension on the peninsula measureably.

Regionalism: The ASEAN Example

The emergence of the Association of Southeast Asian Nations (ASEAN) as a vibrant and meaningful regional force has been one of the significant developments in Asia in recent years. The five nations involved—Indonesia, Malaysia, the Philippines, Singapore, and Thailand—have a combined population larger than ours, totaling some 260 million. Possessed to varying degrees with rich natural resources, growing skilled-labor forces, and rapidly developing economies, these nations have been working together on a number of political and economic fronts to present a united stance to the rest of the region and the world. Little noticed at first, ASEAN has become a potent force, one that is increasingly paid attention to in international forums.

As Lawrence B. Krause, Senior Fellow at the Brookings Institution and an individual well versed in the growth of ASEAN and particularly suited to draw a judgment about it, put it:

> ASEAN is the most important political and economic development in the world since the creation of the European Common Market and deserves great support. I think it is very important both to the United States and to the member countries. The five ASEAN nations are among the fastest growing countries in the world and have a larger total population than the United States. They have a faster growth rate on average than Japan in the last 15 years. Thus it is a tremendous market for the U.S., and is also a potential supplier of many products. Their geographic position is critical in a political-security sense, and ASEAN has been useful in sustaining the political strategy of all these countries in a very trying time.

As an organization, ASEAN has served to reduce the potential for conflicts among its member states. The stronger it becomes, furthermore, the less likely is the possibility of outside interference and exploitation. Its common stance in the face of the Vietnamese expulsion of the wave of refugees—the "boat people"—was an example of this. Both Vietnamese and Soviet diplomatic efforts have been met with the kind of united voice that was impossible before.

Overall, many of the political and economic goals of the ASEAN nations are basically compatible with our own. They preserve the essential neutrality of some of the world's most important sea lanes. Although U.S. and ASEAN interests will not always be the same, these countries represent societies with many values and aspirations that deserve our understanding and support. In giving that support, the United States should listen to, deal with, and consult seriously with the ASEAN nations as a group. The recent creation of the ASEAN-U.S. Trade Council was an appropriate and timely step in this regard. We should not push our presence but let ASEAN grow from within as a local regional organization, thereby averting suspicions among ASEAN members of potential U.S. or Japanese domination.

Nor should there by any attempt to turn what is primarily a political and economic entity into a military grouping or even to try to graft on a military adjunct. A moderate U.S. military capability in the region is called for since it helps provide a sense of security given greater immediacy by Vietnamese aggressiveness and a more visible Soviet presence. But ASEAN is not a closet SEATO (Southeast Asia Treaty Organization).

The New Soviet Presence

Throughout these pages we have seen a steady current of dislike for and skepticism about the USSR. Among nations in Asia, it usually brings up the rear in American perceptions, along with Vietnam and North Korea.

Simple anticommunism is not an adequate explanation for these attitudes, given the dramatic reversal in the views of Americans about the People's Republic of China (recognizing, of course, that Soviet observers would question China's ideological credentials). Negative feelings about the Soviet Union are based on other factors—distrust of its people, its leaders, its motives, and concern over its international activities.

The leadership figures we talked with expressed virtually unanimous disquiet about the increased Soviet presence and level of activity in the region, but they were also inclined to treat it with a sense of confidence and belief that Soviet influence has been blown out of proportion and Soviet actions often have proved counterproductive to Soviet interests.

The Soviet role in Vietnam, for example, has served to help solidify ASEAN. The buildup of Soviet military forces on the northern islands off the coast of Japan (which are still claimed by Japan) has encouraged sentiment favorable to the U.S.-Japan Security Treaty. With China playing a more moderate regional role, the USSR and Vietnam (the latter closely linked to the former, if not its proxy or surrogate) have come to be seen as the principal threats to peace in the area. Their activities are suspect, and exploitable.

There is, it should be mentioned, a certain irony in the path that history has taken in recent years in Asia. The adversarial picture that had once been assumed to be both inevitable and immutable—struggle between communist and noncommunist nations, with the USSR, China, North Korea, and North Vietnam a core against the noncommunist world—turned out to be a chimera. Now the chief protagonists are the communist nations themselves, an outcome hardly to be expected.

This has presented countries in Asia and the United States with unanticipated and substantial opportunities. Given the uncertainty surrounding Soviet and Vietnamese activities, it is important that the United States retain its military superiority in the region. Our commitment to the area, and to the vital U.S. interests involved, need to be enunciated in clear and unequivocal terms. For our friends, it provides a necessary sense of security. For our adversaries, it provides a necessary warning and statement of purpose so that they will not take foolish risks.

In countering the new and expanded Soviet presence, some broad guidelines may be considered. The United States should help to build up and strengthen the economies of those countries that wish to remain outside Soviet domination. As we help to ensure them an alternative, so will the USSR hold less appeal. But this sense of rivalry does not mean that Soviet presence in the region should be used as an opening wedge to turn every disagreement into a local extension of the larger U.S.-Soviet test of wills. The USSR cannot be banished from Asia, and if American policy becomes, or appears to become, obsessively focused on such a goal, the United States surely will lose credibility. And however unrealistic the effort may seem, we should try, wherever possible, to convince Moscow that it is in its own best interests to be more constructive in the region. Its substantial failures to date might even serve to give Moscow pause as to the ultimate efficacy of the policies it has been pursuing.

Notes

1. See William Watts and Lloyd A. Free, "Nationalism, Not Isolationism," *Foreign Policy,* fall 1976, pp. 3–26, and Watts and Free, "Internationalism Comes of Age—Again," *Public Opinion,* April/May 1980, pp. 46–50.

2. See William Watts and Lloyd A. Free, *State of the Nation III,* (Lexington, Mass.: Lexington Books, D.C. Heath, 1978), 1978, pp. 129–134; William Watts, George R. Packard, Ralph N. Clough, and Robert B. Oxnam, *Japan, Korea, and China,* (Lexington, Mass.: Lexington Books, D.C. Heath, 1979), pp. 38–40; and Richard L. Sneider and William Watts, *The United States and Korea,* Potomac Associates, 1980, pp. 14–17.

`3. The reader will note that the 1980 figures for defense of major European allies and Japan are even more supportive here than in the questions pertaining to internationalism and isolationism, discussed in the preceding section. The responses came from two different surveys: February of 1980 for the preceding data in a special study carried out for the magazine *Public Opinion* and July of 1980 for data in table 6–1 as part of the general survey funded by the Luce Foundation for this book.

7 Summary

The overall image that Americans have of Asia is highly varied. That is only fitting since Asia is a region of extraordinary complexity, richly diverse in its lands, cultures, and peoples, and impossible to encapsulate in simple universally applicable terms.

I believe, nonetheless, that the preceding pages have shown that substantial misinformation about Asia and its nations does abound. Negative stereotypes about the area as a whole dominate—an assessment, to be sure, not without justification if we consider that overcrowding, underdevelopment, and political instability have been the reality in many Asian lands. But, as we have seen, these stereotypes are applied indiscriminately to specific lands and peoples, suggesting that many of the remarkable and explosive changes taking place in that part of the world have not yet been fully understood or even heard of by many of our citizens.

Also, as we have seen, opinion about Asia, or certainly most of the countries in the region, tends to be hazy and unstructured. Respondents in our survey frequently chose the most noncommittal and neutral of options where this opportunity presented itself, while the number of "do not know" answers was in many instances rather high. On some relatively straightforward information queries, proportions of those who were mistaken were strikingly large.

These statements are something of an oversimplification, but they do correspond to a number of the general trends we have found. Let us, then, go a bit further, keeping in mind in particular the comparative ratings that Americans gave the nations of Asia for a number of basic attitudinal measurements—feelings of warmth or hostility toward countries in the region, evaluation of the quality of products that they produce, the sense that Americans have of the standard of living in these lands, and the degree of political stability they are thought to possess. All these ratings have been drawn together in tables 7-1 and 7-2, which show the total favorable ratings

Table 7–1
Composite Table: Total Favorable Ratings (+ 1 to + 5)

	Like/ Dislike		Quality of Life		Political Stability		Quality of Products	
Canada	95	(1)	94	(1)	92	(1)	94	(1)
Australia	91	(2)	90	(2)	86	(2)	84	(4)
Japan	84	(3)	81	(4)	85	(3)	86	(3)
New Zealand	83	(4)	80	(5)	77	(7)	75	(6)
West Germany	81	(5)	86	(3)	81	(4)	87	(2)
Brazil	81	(5)	73	(7)	69	(10)	77	(5)
Philippines	80	(7)	67	(8)	68	(11)	74	(7)
Israel	78	(8)	75	(6)	71	(9)	74	(7)
China	70	(9)	55	(9)	78	(5)	74	(7)
Taiwan	68	(10)	54	(11)	56	(13)	65	(11)
Singapore	66	(11)	47	(13)	60	(12)	57	(12)
India	63	(12)	27	(19)	51	(14)	54	(13)
South Korea	59	(13)	40	(14)	37	(18)	53	(14)
Thailand	59	(13)	35	(15)	43	(15)	52	(15)
Indonesia	57	(15)	33	(16)	43	(15)	47	(16)
Malaysia	56	(16)	30	(18)	41	(17)	45	(17)
Saudi Arabia	55	(17)	55	(9)	78	(5)	70	(10)
Nigeria	54	(18)	32	(17)	36	(19)	44	(19)
Vietnam	28	(19)	14	(21)	22	(21)	28	(21)
North Korea	26	(20)	23	(20)	35	(20)	31	(20)
USSR	23	(21)	49	(12)	73	(8)	45	(17)

Note: Numbers in parentheses indicate rank order of countries in each category.

Table 7–2
Composite Table: Highly Favorable Ratings (+ 4 to + 5)

	Like/ Dislike		Quality of Life		Political Stability		Quality of Products	
Canada	75	(1)	70	(1)	68	(1)	54	(1)
Australia	49	(2)	47	(2)	52	(2)	29	(4)
West Germany	33	(3)	40	(3)	40	(3)	48	(3)
Japan	30	(4)	33	(4)	39	(4)	49	(2)
New Zealand	28	(5)	22	(5)	32	(6)	17	(7)
Israel	28	(5)	18	(6)	24	(8)	21	(5)
Brazil	21	(7)	14	(7)	16	(9)	18	(6)
Philippines	21	(7)	10	(9)	15	(10)	11	(11)
China	17	(9)	8	(11)	29	(7)	14	(9)
Saudi Arabia	15	(10)	12	(8)	13	(11)	15	(8)
Taiwan	13	(11)	6	(12)	10	(12)	12	(10)
Singapore	9	(12)	5	(13)	10	(12)	6	(14)
India	9	(12)	2	(17)	6	(15)	8	(12)
Thailand	9	(12)	4	(14)	5	(16)	6	(14)
South Korea	9	(12)	3	(15)	5	(16)	6	(14)
Nigeria	7	(16)	3	(15)	4	(18)	4	(18)
USSR	6	(17)	9	(10)	36	(5)	8	(12)
Indonesia	5	(18)	2	(17)	3	(18)	5	(17)
Malaysia	5	(18)	2	(17)	3	(19)	4	(18)
Vietnam	5	(18)	2	(17)	3	(19)	3	(20)
North Korea	2	(21)	2	(17)	7	(14)	2	(21)

Note: Numbers in parentheses indicate rank order of countries in each category.

and only the highly favorable ratings for each country, respectively. The numbers in parentheses in each table represent the rank order in that category.

Americans are prone to give especially high ratings to two countries in the region: Australia, with (like us) its predominantly English heritage, enhanced by a frontier image (the "outback") and pioneer spirit reminiscent of the American past; and Japan, home of the new "Asian Yankees," hard-working, entrepreneurial, supplying us with manufactured goods of the highest quality—somewhat threatening, to be sure, but still the object of much grudging admiration.

At the other end of the scale are three countries that Americans in large numbers disdain: North Korea, Vietnam, and the USSR. Their unpopularity was in evidence at almost every turn in the results of our survey. Generally disliked, they are seen as aggressive, deceitful, producers of shoddy goods, and, especially in the case of North Korea and Vietman, politically unstable and suffering from a poor standard of living.

Insofar as the countries in between are concerned, by far the most striking feature is the impressive surge of positive feelings toward China. Americans, it would appear, have come not only to accept our new and expanding bilateral relationship but to revel in it. This China euphoria, however, brings with it certain imponderables that will have to be sorted out and that will surely engender disappointments and discord along the way, as the relationship unfolds and matures. One of those uncertainties is the future of Taiwan and its people, for whom Americans continue to hold reasonably positive views and who do not appear to have been forgotten in the rush of enthusiasm over the glamorous opening with the People's Republic.

Among other countries in the middle, the Philippines ranks rather well in American perceptions—surprisingly so, some would say, given the limited but still rather pointed reporting on domestic unrest and allegations of violations in the area of human rights. South Korea, on the other hand, has been damaged by a severe image problem, reflected until Ronald Reagan's assumption of the presidency in greatly strained official relations, even as economic ties between the United States and Korea flourished.

For many Americans, the rest of Asia is something of a mystery. When respondents were asked to assess their knowledge of countries in the region, 20 percent or more said they knew "nothing at all" about Malaysia, Indonesia, Singapore, New Zealand, and Cambodia. If we combine those who said they know "nothing at all" with

those who said they knew "not very much" about each of the countries in question, then majorities of Americans felt this way about
these five countries—plus Thailand, North Korea, Taiwan, South
Korea, and the Philippines. There is, in short, a great perceptual
void: opinion is unsure and unformed, although surely susceptible to
considerable movement for better or worse.

This range of opinion was reflected in the degree of commitment
Americans showed for coming to the defense of certain countries.
Those countries at or near the top of other relative assessments—
Japan and Australia—do well, with such support expressed by very
substantial majorities. So also does the Philippines, a country in the
middle but tending upward in the ratings, and boosted by many
Americans' awareness of its past colonial link with the United States
and its strategic importance due to the presence of U.S. military
bases on its territory. But the situation differs for three other lands:
Taiwan, enmeshed in the new American fascination with China;
Thailand, little known except in relation to a refugee and border
problem in which Americans have little abiding interest and which
probably worries them as opening the door to "another Vietnam;"
and South Korea, seen as an unpopular aid recipient, politically
unstable, and, when covered in the American media, generally
reported in negative and problem-laden terms. All find support for
their defense much more tenuous, with the barest of pluralities in
favor for Taiwan, and slight majorities opposed in the cases of South
Korea and Thailand.

Economically, of course, Asia is perceived overwhelmingly in
terms of Japan, the subject of admiration but also concern. As a
threat to American jobs, it is far ahead of the field, followed at some
distance by Taiwan, while China begins to loom over the horizon.

The fascinating portrait that emerged from our broad national
survey was substantially modified and enriched by probing discussions with a number of individuals who have given much of their
time, energies, and expertise over the years to dealing with Asia. As
we have seen, their views consistently placed Asia in much sharper
focus, underlining its crucial importance to the United States (and
ours to it), its enormous actual and even greater potential wealth in
terms of natural and human resources and capacities, and the need to
place Asia more squarely in the center of our national radar screen.

It is time to try to bring together this unique combination of lay
and expert reactions, perceptions, attitudes, and ideas, combined

with extensive discussions undertaken by the author on both sides of the Pacific, into a policy-related agenda. Such an agenda needs to think in terms both of official governmental activities, on one hand, and private, nonofficial actions, on the other. These frequently overlap or must be approached either cooperatively or jointly. And there is much room for action both here and in Asia.

8 America and Asia: An Agenda for the Future

No one book can present a comprehensive set of proposals and policy recommendations that would satisfy all readers and all needs. I hope that in the preceding pages we have looked at some of the right questions and addressed some of the most enduring issues, making possible a listing of appropriate and feasible suggestions.

I have divided this agenda into four sections (followed by some closing observations): possible actions by the U.S. government, by the American private sector, by interested governments in Asia, and by the private sector in interested Asian nations. Some of the recommendations made here have appeared in earlier pages but are repeated for the sake of completeness.

An Agenda for the U.S. Government

Let us first look at some general areas of concern.

1. More than any one person, the president of the United States can play a major role in setting U.S. policy for Asia, in helping Americans become aware of the realities of Asia in the world, and in explaining the importance of Asia and its impact on the conduct of our foreign policy and, indirectly, the conduct of our everyday lives. By moving Asia to a higher place on his agenda, the president can send a signal that will be felt not just in the executive branch of the U.S. government but on Capitol Hill and throughout the entire political, educational, and economic fabric of our society. Asia regularly receives secondary billing in such keystone presidential speeches and statements as the "State of the Union" address (unless we are involved in a major war in Asia); presidential trips to Asia occur with far less frequency than do such journeys to Europe; and the conduct of our relations with many countries in Asia often appears dominated by a desire for "spectaculars" rather than for the development of the workmanlike, albeit still friction-laden, relationship

that generally characterizes our dealings with many countries in Western Europe.

A reordering, or at least better balancing, of priorities seems in order here.

At the highest level, this means an effort on the part of the president and his principal staff and advisors to dignify our dealings with Asian countries with the same kind of respect and equality of approach (a "horizontal relationship," some have suggested) that suffuse our ongoing relations with most nations in Europe. It means more open consultations on key policy questions. It means an end to the kind of "shocks" that we as a government have administered with remarkable regularity to key friends in Asia, informing them only at (or even after) the event when we decide on a substantial or even momentous policy departure.

The president—any president—should make clear both by his words and actions the importance of Asia to the United States. This is not to place Asia out of proportion in terms of American global interests but to give it proper balance and emphasis. What is required is a degree of subtlety and sophistication at the presidential level in our dealings with the nations of Asia that has all too often been lacking in the past.

2. Correspondingly, Americans need to be more fully apprised of the nature and extent of our security interest—again a task that is presidential in scope. While strong support is shown for the defense of Japan, Australia, and the Philippines, the lukewarmness of such support elsewhere suggests a serious lack of understanding of just where American interests lie. This is certainly true in the case of South Korea: very real concerns over the course of political developments there are legitimate, but the fact remains that Korea's security relates closely to that of Japan and the entire region—and thus to our own.

In addition, the nature of the Soviet presence in Asia, given growing Soviet potential as a Pacific naval power that could disrupt vital sea lanes, needs to be examined and explained more fully. If the Straits of Hormuz have been absent from the standard geographic framework of most Americans, what about the Straits of Malacca?

The president then must convey clearly to the American people, and to friend and adversary alike in Asia, that we have fundamental economic, political, and security interests in the region, that we have enduring ties with nations that have a common interest in freedom and stability, that we must and will maintain an appropriate military presence in the region to protect these basic beliefs, and that we are in it for the long term. No single American can speak to these commitments with the same authority and credibility that are the president's. Once again, tact and restraint are called for so as not to appear unduly aggressive or making too much of the Soviet threat (many Asians believe we overstate it). But friendly nations do need to know that our commitments are durable and that we can truly be relied on.

3. As part of a considered stance of respect for Asia and Asian countries that accords with that which we show Europe, every effort should be made for the highest level of attendance at all appropriate meetings. This does not mean that the president or his principal cabinet officers must shuttle off across the Pacific at a moment's notice. It does mean that major Asian ministerial conferences, including but not limited to ASEAN and ANZUS (Australia-New Zealand-United States) gatherings, should have U.S. representation at a level commensurate with that from other participating nations. It is a mark of respect and interest that will be appreciated, and that will allow the development of personal ties that can be invaluable at later moments of friction.

4. Mention of ASEAN and ANZUS brings to the fore another aspect of a widespread tendency of American officials—to think of Asia primarily, if not exclusively, in terms of Japan, China, and the USSR. Other countries in the region are also extremely important to us and we to them. It behooves U.S. officials not to focus too narrowly on a single triad but to think more of the region as a whole.

5. Every possible effort should be made within the executive branch to bring into government service, and use properly, persons of genuine Asian expertise, as well as to make the best use of the most qualified individuals already in the government. Selection of ambassadors is a sensitive and important task. The functions of these men and women are such that appointments should not be made as a form of political reward. Foreign governments may accede to the naming of a friend of the president who is being given a diplomatic plum in return for loyal service, long companionship, or a bountiful checkbook. That is not to say, however, that those governments enjoy being the host for such an individual, if his training and range of interests do not qualify him in any reasonable way for the job. While diplomacy has been changed enormously by modern communications and the desire (and ability) of presidents and their key advisors

to handle many issues directly and privately with their foreign counterparts, the fact remains that the American ambassador has a vital and difficult role to play. People asked to take on such duties should be of the highest intellectual and moral caliber, commanding the respect they deserve and will need in times of trouble.

A few comments are in order here on a country-by-country, or regional, basis, dealing at a more specific level and moving below the day-to-day purview of the White House. It is not the intent to spell out a detailed policy agenda for U.S. relations with each country in the region. Experts are in place for that, working with a required degree of detail and current knowledge.

6. The centerpiece of U.S. policy in Asia is our relationship with Japan. But this relationship has been troubled by continuing points of friction in the economic sphere, by official U.S. impatience with Japan's unwillingness (or, as many Japanese would see it, political inability) to augment its contribution in the defense and security field, and by insensitive actions taken on both sides from time to time that have raised hackles on one side of the Pacific or the other.

Without being unduly optimistic, it seems fair to say that the very fact that these problems have been increasingly aired—not always in fruitful fashion but not always in contentious fashion, either—is a step in the right direction. Some of the most skilled and respected negotiators in both governments, as well as respected and highly knowledgable people outside of government but with vast experience in each other's country, have been put to work trying to find solutions or at least paths of amelioration. They must be encouraged in their efforts, without undue niggling and calls for advantage by special interest groups on either side.

It would be particularly helpful if more ways could be explored to put the focus on areas of common interest rather than on bilateral frictions. Partly because of the tendency in U.S. official circles to keep our eyes on targets elsewhere, some problems with Japan get blown out of proportion because of prior neglect. Continuing working groups, both bilateral and multilateral (to include the European Economic Community, which also has an enormous stake in Japan) could help defuse potential areas of disagreement by acting as a kind of early-warning system. We have too much to gain through an open and mutually supportive relationship to risk having it soured by an unnessary growth of misunderstandings that could lead to genuine mistrust.

7. Americans, as we have seen, accept and increasingly value our expanding relationship with the People's Republic of China. Particularly on the part of those who have dealt extensively at first hand with Beijing, however, there is a strong sense of caution as to how far, and especially how fast, it is in our interest to go in developing this new link. Ties with China should be explored and augmented primarily on their own merits, keeping a sharp weather eye on what is happening inside China and on how our dealings with it affect our relations elsewhere.

To some degree, the pace with which we expand our China connection is dependent on Soviet activities—especially the augmentation of Soviet naval strength in the region and the buildup of Soviet ground forces in north Asia. But our concern over Soviet activities should not be such that we let our China policy become hostage to Moscow. The nature of our political and economic links with China is more important than any actual or, for the forseeable future, potential military relationship. That being the case, we should move with caution and with our own enlightened self-interest very much in mind, not rushing too precipitately to fulfill perceived Chinese desires and not losing our own freedom of action.

One aspect of that freedom of action is how the United States treats relations with Taiwan and the fulfillment of pledges made on behalf of its people over several decades. The suspicion lingers that even the authorities in Beijing look on our handling of this question as a touchstone of the reliability and constancy of the American connection. Surely others in Asia, and elsewhere in the world, will do so—concluding that, if we abandon our commitment to Taiwan after so much international and domestic turmoil, the American word might as well be discounted in many other circumstances. The ultimate solution of this issue is one for Beijing and Taipei to resolve, to be sure. After all, Americans and all other Westerners who dealt with China in the worst days of foreign exploitation always fell back on Chinese (the "compradores") to act as middle men in their dealings with the authorities of their day, so why should we be any better able to interpose a solution now? But until that solution is forged, in whatever Chinese fashion it may be done, we must insist that the rights of the people of Taiwan be heard and respected. Anything short of that would be just cause for forfeit of any respect due us on this unusually complicated and sensitive issue.

8. ASEAN deserves American support. As mentioned earlier, we

should make sure that the United States is appropriately represented at major ASEAN conferences or meetings at which U.S. presence is requested. But the U.S. role should be one of interest, involvement, and respect, without any indication of a desire to dominate or act as a partner of undue influence.

The United States can undertake a number of official steps that could be well received by ASEAN nations. These include traditional forms of direct aid, where requested, programs of technological transfer to assist ASEAN development, and specific projects of direct interest in the region—development of a common coast guard against smuggling, new approaches to energy production, and another round of efforts to increase food output.

9. The need was stated earlier for clarifying the long-term nature of the U.S. commitment to peace and stability in Asia, including the Korean peninsula. And, as noted, given the overall lack of support among Americans for such a commitment in Korea, it is vital that the regime in P'yongyang have no false illusions about its ability to resort once again to arms without having to worry about an immediate U.S. response. The United States must, in short, sustain its position in South Korea, even while it pushes for any opening of a North-South dialogue, using whatever leverage it possesses with Japan, China, and the USSR to promote such an exchange.

We should also continue to press South Korea to do its fullest in terms of military burden sharing, both to ease our own burden and, as a possible side-effect, to improve the generally negative image that so many Americans have of Korea. (It is also possible that Japan could contribute to this burden-sharing effort in Korea; by helping to underwrite the costs of U.S. forces there, it might also ease one of the major strains in U.S.-Japan relations.)

It is appropriate for the United States to make known its hope and expectation that South Korea will move steadily along the path of institutionalization of civilian rule and of protection of civil safeguards, threats to which have soured our bilateral relations in the past. This is an area where subtlety, sensitivity, and tact are called for in the highest degree and where the loudest voice is not necessarily the most effective.

10. One aspect of dealing with the increased Soviet presense in the region that has not been touched on is the nature of our relation-ship—or lack of it—with Vietnam. Americans were badly seared by our experience in that country, but we have emerged from that par-

ticular trauma with a renewed sense of commitment to at least some of our friends in Asia.

Much of the Soviet position in Asia depends on its close ties with Vietnam. As long as Vietnam has no alternative to Soviet economic, as well as political and security, support, it will have no incentive to ease its bellicosity and play a more constructive role in Southeast Asia. Keeping that in mind, and recognizing as well the political reality represented by the very considerable antipathy Americans now have toward Vietnam and its people, it only makes sense for the United States to keep open the possibility of charting a new policy toward Vietnam—one that would at least ease its dependence on the Soviet Union. A Vietnam less closely aligned with the Soviet Union would also be a Vietnam possibly less threatening to the other countries in the region—Cambodia, to be sure, excluded.

11. Cambodia itself presents the saddest and most shameful of all problems with which the United States must deal on the Asian scene—sad and shameful because of our own responsibility for the present plight of that ravaged land. Arguments have been, and will continue to be, made as to where the ultimate responsibility lies, with those most closely involved at the time having their own views. Suffice it to say that the United States must continue to seek a neutralization of Cambodia that will permit what is left of that civilization to regain its identity and way of life. Its refugees, like those from Vietnam, deserve our support and assistance as the most obvious representation of the ideal of a human-rights policy—an ideal that does spring from the best side of the American character and that can find ready expression in the cause of these refugees.

12. Because of the high regard Americans hold for Australia and the overall absence of problems in our relationship with the "land down under" and its neighbor, New Zealand, it is easy to overlook the very substantial nature of our relationship with these two nations. The fact is that our treaty alliance, the ANZUS tie that is taken so much for granted in the United States, is a major contributor to stability in the region and provides us and our friends with an important link in a vital global communications and security network. But Americans need to be reminded of just how important that link is and how valuable the warm and open ties we have with these two nations are. As with ASEAN, we should make sure to give ANZUS the respect it deserves and not ignore or underrate such a major asset.

13. Finally, in this regional context, the U.S. government should

stand ready to listen to legitimate requests for assistance from any of our friends in the area. These might include calls for military aid from Thailand, military training there or elsewhere, or continued and expanded use of the PL 480 program.

There are a variety of other actions that the U.S. government can undertake to strengthen our overall understanding of Asia and to improve our relations with its countries.

14. Not only should the president and his principal advisors include Asia on their travel agenda but so should concerned members of Congress. Parliamentary exchange is an important way of establishing more open channels of communication and of creating personal links and direct levels of understanding of enormous educational value. Conference facilities are available throughout the region, or at the East/West Center in Hawaii, and should be used to the fullest.

15. Given the magnitude of economic and developmental problems that exist in the region, the United States should fulfill its commitments to the International Bank for Reconstruction and Development (the World Bank) and the Asian Development Bank. In a period of stringency and budget cutting at home, these are easy targets, without much of a vocal and effective constituency. But investments in these major lending institutions have a huge potential for payoff; it is in our interest to make sure they can continue to do their work and promote better standards of living and stability in the region.

16. Also on the economic front, the U.S. government, most importantly through the Department of Commerce, should play a more active role in export promotion. Many segments of the U.S. economy are not strongly export oriented; some that are, are not adequately effective. The foreign commercial service in the Commerce Department has an important role to play here, and efforts should be made to recruit the best possible people for service in its ranks. The department can also do a more aggressive job in the field of public information, helping to make Americans better aware of opportunities that the Asian region holds and contributions it makes to our own economic well-being.

17. Debate continues on just how open some of the markets in Asia really are. Japan, in particular, has come under heavy criticism in recent years for allegedly setting up a number of invisible or hardly

visible barriers that make it difficult for American businessmen to ply their trade successfully. Excessive customs checks, refusal (never acknowledged) to purchase goods of foreign manufacture, specification requirements of extraordinary detail—these and similar devices have reputedly been resorted to in order to limit, if not totally stifle, outside competition.

Whatever the truth of these accusations (in the case of Japan, steps to remove some nontariff barriers affirm their prior existence), it is certainly the proper role of the U.S. government to look into complaints registered by its citizens, and, if they are found to be valid, then to press the government in question to abide by accepted rules of international commerce. Countries where infractions of this kind prevail should understand that if they want American capital investment, technology, and market access, then they must accord similar access to their own.

18. The reverse of this proposition holds true as well. In spite of numerous and, in some quarters, very strong, calls for protectionist measures to limit foreign competition in this country, the larger interests of our citizens will be best served by avoidance of severe protectionist legislation. The opening wedges are already in place, with agreement (reluctantly) by some foreign exporters to quotas or "orderly marketing agreements." The most effective long-term course for American enterprises that are threatened by foreign imports is modernization, retooling, increased labor productivity, and a return to the levels of efficiency for which the American worker once was renowned.

Domestic political realities being what they are, some of the restrictions just referred to are bound to endure, although their duration is unclear. But as long as they are in place, American leverage against foreign governments that restrict directly or indirectly our commercial activities in their countries is bound to be reduced.

19. American businessmen and others with activities in Asia (or in other parts of the world, for that matter) frequently complain that a variety of rules and regulations enacted by Congress or placed in effect by executive order over the years have served to hamper, sometimes severely, their functioning overseas. Some examples of such allegedly restrictive legislation or statutes that many Americans would like to see modified or revoked include: the Foreign Corrupt Practices Act; certain tax laws as they are applied to Americans living

abroad and which, by counting some benefits as earned income (education and rent costs, for example) can make their assignments prohibitively expensive to the employer; application of U.S. antitrust laws abroad; and human-rights riders that can restrict official or unofficial activities.

At the very least, either the executive or the legislative branch, or both, should look into the legitimacy of the complaints against these and other statutes on the books, and consider whether they should be amended or stricken entirely. There is little point in shooting ourselves in the foot.

20. Various federal support programs have been critically important in advancing Asian language and area studies in the United States. The highly respected Fulbright student-exchange program, for instance, has opened the eyes and minds of many Americans to other lands and cultures. The National Defense Education Act has provided critical assistance to language and area studies. The National Endowment for the Humanities has greatly enhanced the activities of such groups as the Asia Society.

Cutting federal funding for programs of this kind is surely shortsighted. We need more people trained in the languages and cultures of foreign lands, Asia included, and restriction of their ability to get such training is absolutely contrary to the national interest. As the report of the President's Commission on Foreign Languages and International Studies (the so-called Perkins Report, named after its director, Dr. James Perkins, former president of Cornell University) put it, we face "a serious deterioration in this country's language and research capacity, at a time when an increasingly hazardous international military, political and economic environment is making unprecedented demands on America's resources, intellectual capacity, and public sensitivity." The "Perkins Commission" further asserted: "Nothing less is at issue than the nation's security. At a time when the resurgent forces of nationalism and of ethnic and linguistic consciousness so directly affect global realities, the United States requires far more reliable capacities to communicate with its allies, analyze the behavior of potential adversaries, and earn the trust and sympathies of the uncommitted."

The need is clear, and should be met. The U.S. government must contribute its share.

21. We noted the awareness of many Americans of a growth in the number of persons of Asian descent in their neighborhoods. The increase in the number of Asians in this country has been, as Census

Bureau figures made clear, impressive. Many of these individuals constitute a human resource that has not been sufficiently or wisely tapped. Certainly in many agencies and bureaus of the U.S. government there is room for Asians, who can bring to bear a direct knowledge of their own country and the area in general on a broad range of questions.

It is worth noting in this regard that much attention is paid at the federal level to adequate placement of black Americans and Americans of Hispanic descent in positions of importance and influence. Given the size and vitality of the American stake in Asia, should not greater consideration be given to utilizing the skills of Asian-Americans for the benefit of our society as a whole?

An Agenda for the American Private Sector

There are at least three major segments within the private sector that can undertake new, or augment ongoing, activities: business, the educational and foundation world, and the media.

For the business community, a variety of actions are possible.

1. In spite of complaints of harrassment and exclusion, many American businesses have been hurt in Asia through lack of preparation and aggressiveness. A much larger investment in training of employees who will be working in Asia is called for, including intensive language and area studies that will give them a better chance to understand the environment in which they will live and operate. And longer tours of duty in the country of assignment would help. It takes time to become established and to learn the local climate, and to be moved on too soon is a waste of knowledge. Expertise is not easily developed and should not be squandered through overly frequent reassignments.

In addition, American corporations often do not display the kind of aggressive efforts at market penetration in Asia that characterize their mode of operation either in the United States or in more familiar cultures in Europe. The ingenuity and competitiveness that they show elsewhere often appears blocked when confronted with substantially different ways of doing business that can be the norm in parts of Asia. Learning to deal with the Japanese trading companies and the highly fractionated Japanese distribution system causes many American businessmen to throw up their hands in despair—

and often cry "foul" when the real problem is lack of understanding.

2. The U.S. business community can also contribute to American awareness of our stake in Asia by turning the talents of American advertising to letting Americans know just how much activity U.S. corporations do carry out in Asia. Many of the imports that we see as threatening to American jobs are made with American materials. Much of the investment that makes some of these imports possible is American. While some of our technolgoy transfer abroad is viewed as coming back to haunt us in the form of foreign growth and domination, much of it is in fact contributing to our high standard of living. If Americans had a better understanding of how much we do get from Asia and how important U.S.-Asian business and commercial ties are to our own well-being, then some of the bias against some Asian lands and peoples could be tempered. Some of the joint U.S.-Asian business groups (Advisory Council on Japan-U.S. Economic Relations, the U.S.-Korea Economic Council, the ASEAN-U.S. Trade Council, and the National Council on U.S.-China Trade, for example) can and do play a highly useful role here.

3. What was said under the agenda for the U.S. government applies every bit as strongly to the business sector. American enterprise needs a massive sense of regeneration and revitalization in the face of very effective foreign competition. With some of the fastest growing economies in the world located in Asia, the challenge to American business is real and is not going to go away. Although calls for protectionist legislation represent an attractive way out, the answer ultimately must come from within. Parts of the American industrial machine need refurbishing, even as other new parts are coming on stream to provide alternatives where American technology and excellence can prevail.

The academic and cultural-informational communities clearly have an enormous responsibility.

4. The American educational system needs a massive infusion of teaching materials, textbooks, and all the growing accoutrements of modern teaching that will help to bring Asia, its land, and its peoples more properly into focus for American students. Particularly at the primary and secondary levels, it is important to give American schoolchildren some awareness of the history, geography, and economic, political, social, and strategic realities of modern Asia. Much of Asia is in rapid transition and is becoming a dynamic global

economic force. Textbooks and classroom presentations need to reflect this new reality and move beyond the Marco Polo image.

5. Related to this is the need for language training. Language and area studies in the Asian field are grossly inadequate in the United States. In almost every Asian country, English-language training is standard, meaning that this resource is built into their overseas capabilities as students come out of school and enter the job market. We lag miserably in this field.

6. Vastly increased teacher exchanges would be most helpful. For American students, the benefits of being taught by a native about his or her country and the region at large are obvious. There is also a great benefit to the American teacher who goes abroad and then returns to impart a new awareness of Asia based on first-hand experience in the region.

7. Components of the educational field, institutions that deal with the vast arena of trying to bring Asia and Asians to America— such as the Asia Society, the Japan Society, local centers such as Japan-American Societies of Washington, Houston, and elsewhere, and many other similar organizations—play a very special and very productive role. They deserve all the support they can get as they carry forward their programs of information, education, training, sponsorship of cultural events, and a wide variety of related activities. Individual benefactors and corporate sponsors should keep these institutions very much in mind as they decide how to allocate their resources. Such organizations make a sustained but not always adequately appreciated contribution to international understanding, awareness, and good will. Some of their ongoing conference activities, such as the Asia Society's Williamsburg meetings that bring together American and Asian leaders for informal but highly productive sessions, provide forums for new ideas and cooperate thinking that have effects far beyond what one might initially think.

The media play the largest single informational role for most Americans, our survey has indicated. That means their responsibility is correspondingly large.

8. It is most unfortunate that at a time when more American correspondents are needed in Asia, soaring costs and, some argue, U.S. tax laws, are forcing newspapers, journals, television and radio networks, and other components of the public media to cut back on overseas operations. If there is any way this trend can be reversed, it should be.

9. For those journalists and others assigned abroad, their hiring organizations should provide, wherever possible, language training before they move to their new posts. If a foreign correspondent in Washington had to rely on a press translation service and local interpreter for virtually all his current news reporting, he would miss much that goes on and work in something of a cultural and intellectual vacuum. Yet this is precisely the case for many (most?) American correspondents in Asia, leaving them open to subtle influences of which they are not even aware. And it certainly hampers their ability to get beyond the obvious and sensational.

10. Overall, in addition, it seems that only rather major crises in Asia will command the attention of those who decide what goes into the principal sources of public awareness about the world. Television, radio, journal, and newspaper editors should make a conscious effort to give increased space to development in Asia, and America's stake in these developments. There needs to be more emphasis on what Asia is all about today and not the heavy focus on student outbursts or human-rights issues, important as they may be. The appeal of television specials such as "Shogun" shows the thirst that many Americans do have for more background about Asia. The continuing remarkable drawing power of "M*A*S*H" also shows the potential that exists for bringing Asia into the thinking of Americans; in this instance, as discussed earlier, it is unfortunate that the image left is so unrelated to the reality of today's Korea.

11. In closing this section, it is worth mentioning again a resource that is becoming increasingly available and which is not yet used nearly as well as it might be—the growing Asian-American community in the United States. In each of the areas just mentioned, Asians can contribute a great deal: as planning officers as well as line personnel in the Asian divisions of major American corporations; as teachers, language instructors, seminar leaders, and curriculum advisors within the American educational system; and as program advisors or news interpreters in our public media. Just as they can contribute to the workings of the U.S. government, so can they bring their own unique talents and experiences to bear within the private sector.

An Agenda for Asian Governments

The principal focus of these pages has been on American perceptions and American activities. I would like, however, to add a few suggestions on actions that Asian governments might consider. These largely apply, of course, to those governments and those countries that are interested in closer and more productive ties with the United States.

1. Those countries in Asia that look to the United States for assistance and support in maintaining their own security against external aggression must also expect continued U.S. pressure for a reasonable sharing of that burden. Particularly as pressures mount on the American budget, it is crucial that friendly governments in Asia recognize the need for them to shoulder responsibility for security to the full extent of their own capabilities.

The most visible target for such pressure has been, as we have discussed already, Japan. Given Japan's extraordinary vulnerability due to its reliance on open-sea lanes for the passage of oil tankers from the Middle East, Japan will be looked to for an enhanced role, regionally limited to be sure, in carrying its own weight in the security equation. Air defense, antisubmarine, and mine-laying competence can all be upgraded, as can practical implementation of the U.S.-Japan Security Treaty.

2. Just as was recommended for the United States, it behooves countries of Asia, to the extent they are concerned with the level of the American presence there—both official and unofficial—to reexamine their policies toward American investment and trade in their territory. Do these policies encourage American investment, and promote American exports across the Pacific, as much as their policies encourage the export of their own commodities to the United States? If not, the possibility of the imposition of protectionist measures by the U.S. government—if the fairness (or lack of fairness) issue becomes overriding—must be taken seriously. If access to American capital, technology, and markets is desired, then reciprocity is mandatory.

3. Asian governments should consider greatly expanded cultural and information programs in the United States. These are long-term undertakings, to be sure, but the potential for significant and positive impact is enormous, as recent highly successful exhibition tours of archeological findings from China and Korea have shown, or as the Japan Today exhibition attests. Such efforts can pay rich dividends, even though the costs and headaches in mounting them are comparably high.

4. Student and teacher exchange and people-to-people programs are as much to the benefit of Asian participants as they are to Ameri-

cans. Since governmental sanction and support is frequently required, it is hoped that such undertakings will receive strong backing from governments in those Asian countries interested in their development—and that the governmental institution involved will provide the appropriate access and assistance to visiting American students, scholars, and teachers that was anticipated in the initial creation of the exchange. Reports from some American participants in China that they have had trouble in gaining access to archives or institutions that they expected would be open to them are disappointing. The history of the U.S.-Soviet exchange program, with which I dealt closely as an embassy officer in Moscow in the early 1960s, has been consistently marred by such problems. Let us hope the same pattern is not reemerging here.

5. Governments of Asia also might consider supporting some of the American institutions that are most involved with promotion of understanding of Asia, such as those mentioned in point 7 in the agenda for the American private sector. Indeed, many governments were generous in supporting the funding drive that made possible the opening of the impressive new Asia Society building in New York City. Such support is both needed and appreciated.

In addition, endowments of university chairs would be most helpful in expanding American understanding of Asia—chairs of Asian studies in general, or for study of the specific donor country. They are badly needed in American institutions of higher learning.

Finally, individual Asian governments might wish to establish in the United States a charitable foundation dedicated to imaginative research, demonstration, and public affairs projects on both sides of the Pacific, thereby promoting intellectual exchange and other cross-fertilization for the advantage of both countries and, quite probably, others as well. A significant example of such an undertaking already exists—the German Marshall Fund of the United States, created as a gift from the Federal Republic of Germany to the United States and the American people in gratitude for American assistance in the economic and political rebirth of West Germany after World War II. It is important to note that this fund operates entirely independently, without influence from German authorities. It has established a respected record in sponsoring a variety of activities that has increased understanding and fostered improved relations between the United States, Germany, and others. Such an endowment could dramatize links between the United States and the donor Asian nation, open the way to a rich range of research, exchange, and other activities among scholars, journalists, technical experts, labor and business leaders, and others, and serve as another link in an emergent chain of partnership.

An Agenda for the Asian Private Sector

To some degree, any suggestions made to the private sector in Asia will mirror what was noted earlier for the American counterparts.

1. For Asian firms doing, or hoping to do, business in the United States, more attention might be paid to the possible benefits of advertising on American television. Heavy television promotion of Japanese products has played a strong role in making Americans more aware of the quantity and quality of Japanese products—concerns about threats to American jobs notwithstanding. The low marks given the quality of products from Taiwan, Singapore, and Korea suggest a basic lack of awareness of what these countries are selling in the United States.

Indeed, in the small and quiet northern Vermont town of Bristol, where most of these pages were written, the largest source of various articles of clothing in the only available store in town—bathing suits, jackets, slickers, shorts, shirts, baseball gloves, sneakers, and so forth—was Asian: Taiwan and Korea. Interestingly, however, virtually nobody with whom I spoke in the store had reflected on this in any meaningful way. Rather, when I pointed out the country of origin of items I was buying, the response tended to be reference to a Japanese commodity that the individual with whom I was speaking owned. And these commodities—television sets, watches, radios, stereo systems, calculators—are all very visible, as is their place of origin. Advertising and visibility go hand in hand.

Just as Asian governments can support American institutions promoting awareness of Asia, so can individuals or corporate entities within the Asian private sector. The dramatic gift in 1981 of a prominent Japanese businessman that made possible the creation of the U.S.-Japan Foundation is but a case in point—not easily replicated to be sure, but an example nonetheless.

3. Last, Asian educational institutions can lend their support to

the growth of student, faculty, and scholarly exchange that has already been touched upon. Some of the great centers of learning are in Asia, and no foreigner visiting the region can fail to be impressed with the passion for learning that is endemic there. Again, the benefits flow both ways.

Ties that Bind

In bringing this book to a close, I would like to leave the reader with two related propositions that flow naturally, I believe, from the discussion and analysis already presented.

On the organizational side, there are a number of movements and activities either already in existence (however nascent), or getting underway, that point to a larger pan-Pacific community. Shortly before his death, the late Japanese Prime Minister Masayoshi Ohira called, for example, for initiatives to create a Pacific Ocean Community. A continuing flow of specific proposals and structural suggestions has emerged from many Pacific nations. These have resulted in a variety of conferences, research projects, and the launching of a number of information and actions groups, which include, in the United States, the Pan-Pacific Community Association. (For an extensive listing of various proposals and activities related to this theme see "Pan-Pacific Community: List of Proposals, Conferences, and Projects," prepared by the Japan Center for International Exchange.)

Given the complexity of the issues involved and the wide range of national and regional interests to be taken into account, it is not surprising that there is continuing debate (and considerable disagreement) as to whether the Pacific community concept should be pursued through private channels, official channels, or both. It is unlikely that this debate has any either/or resolution. Rather, development of a cohesive regional Pacific notion undoubtedly will proceed on all fronts, some maturing faster than others. The fact that much, but not all, of the impetus thus far has come from the United States, Japan, and Australia is not altogether healthy. In particular, strong involvement of ASEAN nations is essential for the ultimate success and durability of whatever structures or programs emerge.

Uncertainties or not, some degree of pan-Pacific regionalism is a goal to be sought and promoted. Its realization could play a significant role in helping to ensure stability, confidence, and greater human welfare throughout the region.

Finally, we turn to a more theoretical consideration—and one that will have particular meaning in the context of mutual dealings between the United States and those nations in Asia that are interested in a long-term, stable, and constructive American presence in Asia.

The overriding reality of future links between the United States and Asia is this: the Pacific connection already has become as important as any other and its importance over the years ahead is bound to increase. That being the case, it would be to the advantage of both sides not to focus so much on the thorny issues that divide, but rather on the common interests that unite. This is not to suggest that we ignore the former; such issues must and will be addressed. But greater emphasis on the latter—the ties that bind—may help create a climate that makes those problems less intractable, and more capable of resolution.

Both of these broad themes represent objectives worth pursuing.

Appendix:
Design
and Composition
of the Sample

The Gallup Organization, which designed the sample used for the field work in this study, maintains a national sample of interviewing areas that is used for all of its National Opinion Trends surveys. The sampling procedure is designed to produce an approximation of the total adult civilian population, eighteen years of age and older, living in the United States, except those persons in institutions such as prisons or hospitals.

The design of the sample was that of a replicated, probability sample, down to the block level in the case of urban areas and to segments of townships in the case of rural areas. Approximately three hundred sampling points—clusters of blocks or rural segments—were used in this survey.

The sample design included stratification by the following seven size-of-community strata: central cities with a population of 1,000,000 and over; of 500,000 to 999,999; of 50,000 to 499,999; the urbanized fringe areas of all of these central cities as a single stratum; cities 2,500 to 49,999; rural villages; and rural open areas. Each of these strata was further stratified into seven geographic regions. Within each city-size regional stratum, the population was geographically ordered and zoned into equal-sized groups of sampling units. A pair of localities was then randomly drawn in each zone with the probability of selection proportional to population size, thus producing two replications.

Within the localities selected for which population data were available, subdivisions were drawn with the probability of selection proportional to size of population. Within each subdivision selected for which block statistics were available, a sample of blocks was drawn with probability of selection proportional to the number of dwelling units. In all other subdivisions or areas, blocks or segments were drawn at random.

In each cluster of selected blocks or segments, a randomly selected starting point was designated on the interviewer's map of the area. Starting at this point, the interviewer followed a specific direction in the selection of households until he completed his assignment. Interviewing was conducted at times when adults in general were most likely to be at home—on weekends and weekdays after 4:00 P.M. for women and 6:00 P.M. for men.

The prestratification by regions was supplemented by fitting each obtained sample to the latest available Census Bureau estimates of the regional distribution of the population. Also, minor adjustments of the sample were made by educational attainment (for men and women separately), derived from the Census Bureau's Current Population Survey.

The composition of the sample in demographic terms is shown in table A-1.

Table A-1
Asia Study: Composition of the Sample

	Number of Interviews	Percentage of Sample (Weighted)
National Totals	1,616	100
Sex		
Men	817	51
Women	799	49
Age		
18–29	406	28
30–49	572	35
50–59	231	14
60 and over	399	23
Undesignated	7	*
Education		
College	557	30
High school	838	54
Grade school	214	16
Undesignated	7	*
Family Income		
$20,000 and over	602	36
$15,000–$19,999	266	16
$10,000–$14,999	328	21
$ 5,000–$9,999	269	16
Under $5,000	137	10
Undesignated	14	1
Occupation		
Professional and business	358	21
White collar	156	10
Manual	471	31
Nonlabor	584	35
Other and undesignated	47	3

Table A-1 continued

	Number of Interviews	Percentage of Sample (Weighted)
Region		
East	467	27
Midwest	465	27
South	424	28
West	260	18
Community Size		
1,000,000 and over	332	20
500,000–999,999	210	13
50,000–499,999	420	25
2,500–49,999	236	15
Under 2,500 and rural	418	27
Race		
White	1,426	87
Black	172	12
Other	18	1
Politics		
Republican	344	21
Democrat	676	41
Independent	542	34
All others	54	4

Most of the demographic categories used in the breakdowns are clear; a few, however, need a word of explanation.

In the case of *education,* "college" included those how have had some college education as well as those who have graduated; the same is true for "high school" and "grade school" (in fact, the latter also includes those few, mostly oldsters, who have had no education at all). *Income* is based on the total earnings of the family as a whole (that is, those members living together in the dwelling where the interview was conducted).

The *occupation* categories are clear except for "nonlabor," which consists primarily of households headed by retired people, or, to a lesser extent, by students, housewives, or the physically handicapped. One of the characteristics of this category is a heavy predominance of older people. Unfortunately, the figures for "farmers" could not be given in the tables noted above because they now represent such a small proportion of our total population that too few were drawn into our sample to provide any degree of statistical reliability.

The different areas under *region* included states as follows: *East:*

Connecticut, Delaware, District of Columbia, Maine, Maryland, Massachusetts, New Hampshire, New Jersey, New York, Pennsylvania, Rhode Island, Vermont, and West Virginia. *Midwest:* Illinois, Indiana, Iowa, Kansas, Michigan, Minnesota, Missouri, Nebraska, North Dakota, Ohio, South Dakota, and Wisconsin. *South:* Alabama, Arkansas, Florida, Georgia, Kentucky, Louisiana, Mississippii, North Carolina, Oklahoma, South Carolina, Tennessee, Texas, and Virginia. *West:* Alaska, Arizona, California, Colorado, Hawaii, Idaho, Montana, Nevada, New Mexico, Oregon, Utah, Washington, and Wyoming.

The categories under *politics* derive from the question, "In politics as of today, do you consider yourself a Republican, Democrat, or Independent?"

Index

Advisory Council on Japan-U.S. economic relations, 104
Afghanistan, Soviet invasion of, 2, 67
Aggressiveness, as characteristic of Asian countries, 26
ANZUS (Australia-New Zealand-United States), 95, 99
Argentina, human rights in, 51
ASEAN (Association of Southeast Asian Nations), xiii, 82-83, 95, 97-98
ASEAN-U.S. Trade Council, 104
Asia: American knowledge of, 11-21; American view of, xi-xiii, xvii-xviii, 1-10; definition, xviii; future relations with the United States, 93-110; human rights in, 48-52; political stability, 44-48; quality of life, 41-44; stereotypes of, 23-39; versus Europe, 1-3, 8-10
Asian language studies, xiv, 102, 105
Asians, immigration of, to the United States, 15-17
Asia Society, 105
Attitudes, American, favorable and unfavorable, 3-7
Australia: American attitudes toward, 4, 5, 89; American defense of, 71; human rights, 48, 50; imports threat to the United States, 60-61; political stability, 45; product quality, 56; quality of life, 41; relations with the United States, 99; as supplier of prime beef, 19; trade with the United States, 53

Australians, characteristics of, American perceptions of, 32, 37

Boat people, 47, 83
Business community, Asia, agenda for, 109-110
Business community, U.S., agenda for, 103-106

California, ethnic communities in, 16
Cambodia: American knowledge of, 11; invasion of, by Vietnam 26; U.S. support of, 99
Canada: American attitude toward, 4, 5; American knowledge of, 11; import threats to U.S., 60-61; product quality, 56
Carter, Jimmy, 48, 51
China: American attitude toward, 5, 89; economic backwardness, 25; importance to U.S. interests, 7; human rights, 49, 50; import threat to the United States, 60; incursion into Vietnam in 1979, 26; modernization, xi; political stability, 45, 47; political upheaval, 25; population, 9; product quality, 57; quality of life, 42, 43; shift in American opinion of, 56, 89, 97; trade with the United States, xvii, 18, 19, 20, 53; U.S. arms to, 77-80
Chinese: American perceptions of, 34-35, 37; immigration of, to the United States, 16
Chung-hee, Park, 35

117

About the Author

William Watts is president of Potomac Associates and a consultant for The Gallup Organization. He also is a professorial lecturer of the Johns Hopkins University School of Advanced International Studies. He has served in the U.S. Foreign Service in Seoul and Moscow, and in the State Department's Office of Asian Communist Affairs and Bureau of Intelligence and Research, Soviet Affairs. He received the M.A. in Russian studies from Harvard University. He is the author or coauthor of numerous articles and books, including *State of the Nation III* (1978) and *Japan, Korea, and China: American Perceptions and Policies* (1979), both published by Lexington Books; and *The United States and China: American Perceptions and Future Alternatives, The United States and Korea: American Attitudes and Policies, The United States and Japan: American Perceptions and Policies,* and *The United States and Korea: New Directions for the '80s.*